SPANISH

Edith Baer
Margaret Wightman

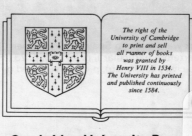

*The right of the
University of Cambridge
to print and sell
all manner of books
was granted by
Henry VIII in 1534.
The University has printed
and published continuously
since 1584.*

Cambridge University Press

Cambridge New York Port Chester Melbourne Sydney

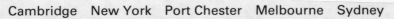

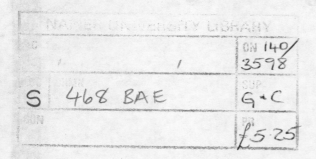

Published by the Press Syndicate of the University of Cambridge
The Pitt Building, Trumpington Street, Cambridge CB2 1RP
40 West 20th Street, New York, NY 10011, USA
10 Stamford Road, Oakleigh, Melbourne 3166, Australia

© Cambridge University Press 1990

First published 1990

Printed in Hong Kong by Wing King Tong Printing Co. Ltd

ISBN 0 521 28193 8

Acknowledgements
The photographs in this book were taken in Spain by Edith Baer,
except for those on p. 24 ('carretera particular'), p. 26 (5d), p. 28 ('zona estacionamiento'),
p. 34 ('Costa Brava', 'guardia civil', 1a, 1e, 2b), p. 35(3) supplied by John Dickinson.

Illustrations by Celia Weber

CE

What this book is about

* It helps you – even if you're a beginner – to understand the signs and notices that will confront you on a visit to Spain. It contains over 600 photos taken throughout Spain.
* It shows you how to get the gist of signs and notices without having to worry about the meaning of every single word.
* It contains plenty of practice material so that you can check your progress.
* It gives you an idea how the Spanish language works.
* It provides some unusual and unexpected insights into the Spanish way of life.

How the book works

'Making sense of signs' gives you some general ideas on how to interpret signs and on how to judge whether they're important to you or not. The chapter includes notes about the way the language on signs works. It tells you which words to look out for and how to sort out the different types of sign.

Chapters 1–14 deal with situations you may have to cope with and the signs you're likely to come across. Each chapter opens with a 'Key words' section which lists those words you'll find most useful. The main part of each chapter contains photos of important signs you'll need, together with explanations. And each chapter ends with 'Test yourself' questions for self-checking.

Word list – at the back of the book – for easy reference and revision.

How to use the book

* First go carefully through 'Making sense of signs'. You can then take the individual chapters in any order – they're self-contained. You may find it a help to re-read 'Making sense of signs' before tackling a new chapter.

* Once you've studied the 'Key words' of the chapter, try to memorise them. Then go on to the section introducing the signs. Concentrate on getting the gist as you would need to in a real-life situation. Resist the temptation to puzzle out every word.

* Finally try the 'Test yourself' questions at the end of the chapter and check your answers with the Key on p. 95.

Contents

4

Making sense of signs

In Spain many areas of public life are well signposted, especially in large towns and tourist resorts. There are signs to warn you, to ask you to do – or not to do – something, to help you on your way and generally to inform you. Spaniards being individualists, there is little uniformity about their signs and notices.

Spanish – or more accurately Castilian – is not the only language used. In Catalonia, the Basque country and Galicia you'll invariably see signs in the local language, sometimes side by side with Spanish. Some of these are included in this book.

You'll often need to get the gist of a sign quickly. Many are written in a style of language that you won't meet in everyday speech. A dictionary won't always help, but guessing may. But there are pitfalls! (see p. 8).

To try and understand every word on a sign or notice can be a waste of effort, so you need to develop a technique to pick out the essentials.

1 Start by concentrating on short bold signs

centro ciudad town centre
entrada camping entrance to campsite

Cachadelos
name of camp

2 Sort out different types of sign

Warnings usually include **atención**, **cuidado**, **precaución** (all meaning 'beware', 'caution') or **peligro** (danger).
  precaución en el baño caution when bathing
  atención al autobús mind the bus

Requests generally begin with words ending in **-a(n)**, **-ar**, **-e(n)**, **-er**, **-ir**, sometimes **-ad**.
  recoja su ticket take your ticket
  empujar push
  respeten el jardín respect (i.e. keep off) the garden

Polite requests say **por favor** (please), **gracias** (thank you), **se ruega** (it is requested) or **le rogamos** (we ask you).
  por favor cierren la puerta please close the door
  le rogamos utilice los carritos please use the trolleys

Signs with **no** usually tell you *not to do* something.

> **no aparcar** no parking
> **no tocar** don't touch

— or inform you that something *isn't* working, isn't happening or isn't available.

> **no funciona** out of order, i.e. not functioning
> **no cerramos a mediodía** we don't close at midday, i.e. lunchtime

Signs with **se prohibe** or **prohibido** *forbid you* to do something.

> **prohibido fumar** no smoking
> **se prohibe acampar** camping prohibited

❓ Test yourself (Answers on p. 95)

Which signs (i) ask you to do something (ii) request you politely to do something (iii) tell you not to do something (iv) forbid you to do something (v) tell you that something is out of order (vi) remind you to take care?

7

3 Pick out the key words

Key words will often help you to decide whether a sign concerns you or not. For instance, if you're looking for the beach a sign with **playa** will be of interest – the rest you can ignore.

la caleta name

You may be able to pick out some words without much difficulty, for example the ones that belong to the same 'family'.

acampar to camp **acampados** campers
aparcar to park **aparcamiento** car park

Many words are guessable.

dentista dentist **museo** museum
limón lemon **reservado** reserved

Watch out for 'false friends' – they look deceptively like English words but mean something entirely different.

autocar coach
cartas letters
normal two-star petrol
particular private
real royal
vía station platform, track

Words ending in **-ción** and **-dad** are particularly treacherous. Some mean practically the same as their English counterparts.

estación station
recepción reception
especialidad speciality
velocidad speed

Others don't!

circulación traffic
exposición exhibition
comodidad convenience (as in 'for your convenience')
localidad seat, ticket

'False friends' are highlighted in the 'Test yourself' section at the end of each chapter. Key words together with related words and expressions are given at the beginning of every chapter.

4 Look for other words that matter

They can also give you a clue what a sign is about and help you to decide whether it affects you or not. Try to memorise the words below – they appear on many signs.

* **abierto** means a place is open

* **aquí** (here) indicates where you get something or should do something.
    aquí tapas variadas choice of bar snacks served here
    pague aquí pay here

* **caja** can be a checkout, cash desk, cashier's or a type of bank

* **cerrado** means a place is closed (look for **tancat** in Catalonia)

* **entrada** (entrance, entry) can also mean admission

* **hay** (there is, there are) tells you that something is available.
    hay café coffee served here
    hay habitaciones rooms available

* **horario** (timetable) alerts you to opening and closing hours, and to times when you may or may not park.
    horario de caja banking hours
    horario limitado limited stay (parking)

* **paso** means 'way' or 'entry'.
    paso prohibido or **prohibido el paso** no entry
    ceda el paso give way

* **perros** (dogs) is a sign you can ignore unless you have a dog with you or the sign is on someone's front gate – then it's a warning, *but* **perros calientes** are 'hot dogs'.
    perros no no dogs
    perro peligroso dangerous dog

estacionamiento parking

* **planta** is a floor or level, but sometimes means what it looks like – 'plant'.

  primera planta first floor
  respetad plantas y flores respect (i.e. don't damage) plants and flowers

* **precio** means 'price' on shopping signs and 'fee' on ticket machines.
  precio fijo fixed price
  precio exacto exact money

* **salida** shows you the way out or indicates the departure of planes, trains, etc.

* **sólo** (only) appears on many parking and admission signs.
  sólo camiones lorries only
  carga y descarga sólo hotel loading and unloading – hotel only

* **Ud.** or **Vd.** (short for **usted**) means 'you' – you see it on signs telling you what to do or where you are.
  sírvase Vd. mismo serve yourself
  Ud. está aquí you're here

❷ Test yourself

Which of these signs would concern you if you (i) wanted to go into a supermarket (ii) wanted to know when a place was open (iii) were looking for a car park (iv) needed accommodation (v) wanted to go to an exhibition

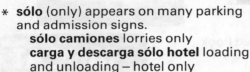

a

b

c

d

e

5 Look at the way the 'sign' language works

Word order

Remember, especially when deciphering short signs, that Spanish word order is often the opposite of English usage.

aparcamiento público public car park
ascensor automático automatic lift
servicio nocturno night service

Words joined by **de** (of) make better sense if you reverse the order and forget about **de**.

estación de servicio service station
día de mercado market day

To shorten signs **de** is often left out.

centro ciudad town centre
jefe (de) estación station master

Or it is written with the E inside the D:

Instructions

Notices telling you politely to do or not to do something usually start with **se ruega** or **le rogamos** (see p. 6). *What* you should or shouldn't do comes next.

le rogamos deposite su bolso en recepción please leave your (shopping) bag at reception
se ruega no tirar cigarrillos al suelo please don't throw cigarettes (i.e. cigarette ends) on the floor

Why you're asked to do something is introduced by **para** (in order to, for).

para evitar molestias to avoid being inconvenienced

Prohibitions

What is prohibited comes after **se prohibe, prohibido** or **no se permite(n), no está permitido** (not allowed).

no se permite la entrada no entry
está totalmente prohibido mariscar gathering shellfish strictly forbidden

To discover *who* isn't allowed to do something look for **a** (for).

prohibido a menores prohibited for minors
prohibido el paso a no acampados no entry for non-campers

How to interpret 'se'

You'll often see it in instructions and prohibitions, meaning 'one'.

se prohibe one forbids, i.e. it is forbidden
se ruega one requests, i.e. it is requested
no se permite one does not allow, i.e. it is not allowed

In other signs **se** tells you that something is being done.

mañana se sortea the lottery is being drawn tomorrow
se alquilan aparcamientos parking spaces to let

Shop signs starting with **se** followed by a word ending in **-an** or **-en** advertise a service.

se hacen llaves keys cut

At the end of a word **se** means 'oneself', 'yourself'.

sírvase serve yourself
no sentarse don't seat yourself, i.e. don't sit down

❷ Test yourself

What are you told to do – or not to do? (Don't try to make sense of every word.)

a

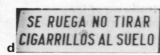

b

c

SE RUEGA NO TIRAR CIGARRILLOS AL SUELO

d

PROHIBIDO EL PASO FINCA PRIVADA

e

6 Recognise different forms of the same word

* An **-s** or **-es** at the end of a word usually tells you that it's plural.

    día day   **estación** station
    días days   **estaciones** stations

    Adjectives follow the same pattern.
    patatas fritas fried potatoes,
    i.e. crisps or chips
    ferrocarriles españoles Spanish
    railways

    Many adjectives end in **-o** (masc.) or **-a** (fem.)
    depending on the words they describe.
    puente romano Roman bridge
    ciudad romana Roman town

churros pieces of dough
fried in oil

* You'll come across various forms for
    'the' **el, la, los, las**
    'of the' **del, de la, de los, de las**
    'to the', 'for the', 'at the' **al, a la, a los, a las**

* A verb can appear in different guises.
    abrir to open   **abierto** open
        abrimos sábado we open on Saturdays

    cerrar to close   **cerrado** closed
        cerramos de 1 a 4 we close from
    1 pm to 4 pm
        cierren la puerta close the door

    rogar to request   **le rogamos** we ask you
        se ruega it is requested

    tocar to touch   **no tocar** }
        no toquen } don't touch

* Accents on **á**, **é**, etc. are used in Spanish for stress. On most signs
    they are left off. But they are always used in the text of this book.

7 Other things you need to recognise

Days of the week

lunes Monday   **los lunes, etc.** 'on Mondays', etc.
martes Tuesday
miércoles Wednesday
jueves Thursday
viernes Friday
sábado Saturday
domingo Sunday
laborables weekdays
festivos public holidays,
sometimes Sundays

misa mass

Times

The 24-hour system is widely used. **H, h, hs, hrs., hras., horas** (hours) mean 'o'clock', so does **las** (short for **las horas**), e.g. **las 2** = 2 o'clock.

With the 12-hour system **mañana** (morning) is often added for 'am', e.g. **7 de la mañana** = 7 am, **tarde** (afternoon, early evening) for 'pm', **noche** for late evening or night.

'Half past' sometimes appears as $\frac{1}{2}$, e.g. **7$\frac{1}{2}$** = 7.30.

'From' is **de**, 'to' is **a**.

oficina office

Numbers

1st, 2nd, 3rd, etc. appear as **1º, 1ª, 2º, 2ª, 3º, 3ª** etc., especially when referring to floors (see p. 17), but they are not used in dates, e.g. **el día 31** (the 31st).

When they refer to a century (**siglo** or **S.**) they look like this: **XV** (15th), **XIX** (19th).

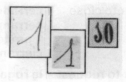

The figure 1 is written in various ways . . .

Money

Prices are given in pesetas: **ptas., pts., p.**

Exclamation marks

It's the Spanish custom to add an 'upside down' exclamation mark at the beginning. To attract your special attention you'll often see more than one!

This sign is at the entrance to a supermarket. What does it say? (Answer on p. 95).

8 Get to know these short words

a	to, for, at	**con**	with
o	or	**por**	through(out), via, because of, for
y	and		
de	of, from	**sin**	without
en	in	**para**	in order to, for

'position closed'

1 Getting around on foot

👤 Key words

calle (street, road)	**calle cortada** road closed **calle sin salida** cul-de-sac **callejón** narrow street
entrada (way in, entrance)	
pasar (to go in or across)	**no pasar** no entry **pase** tells you to enter
paso (way through or across)	**paso inferior** subway **paso prohibido** no entry
	but **paseo** is a tree-lined avenue, often one where Spaniards take their traditional evening stroll
peatón (pedestrian)	**calle peatonal** pedestrian precinct
salida (way out, exit)	**salida de emergencia**, **salida de socorro**, **salida de urgencia** emergency exit

Muiñeira place name
bajada way down

Finding your way

Look for direction signs (usually navy or black on off-white) to find particular places such as the town centre (**centro ciudad** or **centro**), harbour (**puerto**), beach (**playa**), or important buildings like the town hall (**ayuntamiento**), station (**estación**), post office (**correos**), church (**iglesia**), castle (**castillo** or **alcázar**).

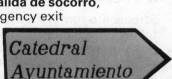

For shopping areas follow **centro comercial**, **mercado** (market, often covered), **hipermercado** (superstore).

abastos provisions

Looking for a street or square

There are many decorative street signs, especially in tourist areas and places of historical interest.

Calle (often shortened to **c.** or **c/**) is the usual name for a street. In Catalonia it's **carrer**. Signs with **calle peatonal** tell you it's a pedestrian precinct, but a street with a sign **calle sin salida** is a dead end.

Callejón is a narrow street.

Other names for streets you'll come across are **avenida** (**av.**, **avd.** or **avda.**), avenue; **paseo** (**po.**), a tree-lined avenue; **pasaje** or **pasadizo**, a passage or alley; **travesía**, a short link between two streets.

Camino tells you that it's a path or way. **Carretera** (**ctra.**) is a main road or roadway. **Plaza** (**plza.**, **pza.** or **pl.**) is a square. **Plaza mayor** means 'main square' and is the focal point of many towns. *But* **plaza de toros** is a bullring.

Calle, **plaza**, etc. are sometimes omitted when it's a well-known street or square. In Madrid, for example, the **plaza de la Cibeles** is called **Cibeles**, the **paseo de la Castellana** is simply **Castellana**. Some street signs bear only the name of a town or a well-known person.

Colón Columbus

Streets are sometimes renamed following a change in local or national government, so be careful if you haven't an up-to-date map. Where there are two signs, the old street name is the one beginning with **antiguo** or **antigua** (former).

Ac. or **Acc.** (short for **accesorio**) after a house number tells you that it's a shop or business premises.

Occasionally you'll see **manzana** on a building – it's not the name of the street, it means 'block'. **Barrio** tells you which district you're in, not which street.

Signs with **pares** (even) and **impares** (odd) show you how the house numbers run.

Génova
name of street

Crossing the road

You may come across traffic lights for pedestrians (**peatones**). Some show the words **pasen** (go) or **esperen** (wait).

To help you to cross (**cruzar**) you may be asked to press (**pulse**) a button (**botón**). Occasionally you're advised to cross (**cruce**) at a certain point or to refrain from crossing (**no cruce**).

Going into places

Entrada marks the entrance or directs you to it.

Where you see **empujar, empuje(n)** or the old-fashioned **empujad** you push the door open. Where it says **tirar, tire(n)** or **tirad** you pull. There may be a sign inviting you to enter without knocking (**sin llamar**) or one drawing your attention to the door bell (**timbre**) or asking you to press the button (**pulsar el botón**), especially when you want to enter a bank.

Pedestrian entrances to a car park (**aparcamiento, parking** or **estacionamiento**) are usually signposted **entrada** or **acceso peatones** or just **peatones**.

Finding your way around buildings

Look at the nameplate outside or the indicator board inside to see whether a particular flat, office, etc., is on the left (**izquierda**, shortened to **izda.**) or on the right (**derecha** or **dcha.**).

On each floor, flats are 'numbered' **A, B, C**, etc. Floors are called **piso** or **planta**. For the 1st floor it may say **primer piso** (**1º**) or **primera planta** (**1ª**), for the 2nd floor **segundo piso** (**2º**) or **segunda planta** (**2ª**), for the third **tercer piso** (**3º**) or **tercera planta** (**3ª**) and so on. **Piso bajo** or **planta baja** (**B** in lifts) means 'ground floor', but the basement is **sótano** (**S** in lifts).

To find the lift look for **ascensor**. **Escalera** (shortened to **esc.**) points the way to the stairs. **Escalera mecánica** is the escalator.

Offices are often marked **oficinas**. Signs with **despacho** direct you to a particular office or room, e.g. **despacho central** (main office), nothing to do with 'despatch'.

Dirección indicates the manager's office, *not* the direction! **Portería** tells you there's a porter's lodge.

To leave a building look for **salida** (exit).

Mind how you go

Avoid going where you see **paso**, **pasar**, **entrada** coupled with **no**, **se prohibe** or **prohibido**, or where it says **privado** or **particular** (private).

This sign is common in the countryside and is intended to keep out campers, poachers and other unauthorised persons.

coto de caza game reserve

On a main road (**carretera**) you frequently see a sign urging you to walk on the left-hand side, that is facing oncoming traffic.

circula walk   **tu** your

Watch out for signs with the old-fashioned ¡**ojo!** (look out! – **ojo** means 'eye'). You find them for instance on an unguarded level crossing (**paso sin guarda**) where it may say **ojo al tren** (mind the train).

Don't ignore signs with **cuidado** or **atención** (beware) and **peligro** (danger). Any mention of **perro(s)** warns you about dogs.

toque ring

❷ Test yourself

Before you attempt the questions go over the chapter again and the 'Making sense of signs' section.

1 Identify these 'false friends':
   antiguo   despacho   dirección   particular   planta   pulse

2 What's the difference between (i) **ciudad – cuidado** (ii) **paso – paseo** (iii) **puerta – puerto**?

3 What kind of streets are these?

a

b

c

4 You've an appointment in **Calle de Génova, 5**. Should you follow this exit?

5 You've just parked your car. What's the message on this sign?

6 Which floor are you on?

a

b

7 You've been recommended this modest hotel. Where do you have to go?

8 Which of the signs below warns you about a dog?

a

b

9 Where do these signs direct you to?

a ENTRADA ALHAMBRA

b P.º DEL PRADO — AUTOBUSES

c CORREOS

d *Iglesia*

e *Estación*

f ESTACIONAMIENTO ALAMEDA VIEJA ACCESO DE PEATONES

10 You may see these signs on doors.
    What do they ask you to do?

c EMPUJAD

a ASCENSOR AUTOMATICO — PULSE LA PLANTA DESEADA

b no pasar

d · PASE SIN LLAMAR ·

11 Which of these are names of streets or squares?

a CALLE PEATONAL

b plaza de toros

c CALLE SIN SALIDA

d MANZANA Nº 183

e Calle REAL

Can that be right?

Mind the milk bottle?!

OJO PINTA

20

2 Motoring

a Going the right way

👤 Key words

auto
(car)

autocar coach *not* car
auto expreso motorail
automóvil motor car
automovilista motorist
autopista motorway
autovía dual carriageway

calle
(street)

calle cebra street where pedestrians have priority
calle peatonal pedestrian precinct
calle sin salida cul-de-sac

carretera
(main road, roadway)

circular
(to drive)

circule(n) drive ..
circulación traffic

paso
(way through or across, right of way)

paso prohibido no entry
paso a nivel level crossing
paso sin guarda unguarded level crossing
al paso at walking pace

sentido
(direction)

cambio de sentido change of direction, turning off (see p. 24).

señal
(sign)

señalización signposting

Symbols worth knowing

road reserved
for motor traffic
(white on blue)

taxi rank – *not*
a cul-de-sac
(white on blue)

to turn left, first
swing right
(white on blue)

on the front of
vehicles: may
be towing a
trailer or
another vehicle
(yellow on blue)

4872 · K

Hiring a car

If you want to hire a car look for **alquiler**
(hire) and **autos** or **automóviles**, or
coches, all meaning 'car' – but
remember **autocar** is a coach, **carro** a trolley.

Self-drive is **sin conductor** (**conductor** = chauffeur).

If you travel by motorail follow the sign **auto expreso**.

AUTOS ALQUILER
CON O SIN CONDUCTOR
BODAS VIAJES

bodas weddings
viajes trips

The rule of the road

Most road sign symbols are the same as in Britain with this exception (yellow on white). It means you're on a main road and have right of way. A dark blue line through it marks the end of the priority.

At most junctions there is a 'stop' sign or one with **paso** (right of way). You must give way where you see **ceda** (yield) **el paso** *but* **prohibido el paso** or **paso prohibido** means 'no entry'.

At crossroads and junctions where there is no sign, traffic from the right has priority.

The colour of direction signs

Most signs are navy or black on off-white. The number on the sign gives you the distance in kilometres.

The road number is in a small panel on or above the sign. A red panel with **N** or **CN** (**carretera nacional**) indicates a trunk road; a Roman numeral means it's one of the trunk roads linking Madrid with other major Spanish cities.

A green panel with **C** (**carretera comarcal**) indicates a main road. A yellow panel tells you it's a local road. It bears the initials of the province or the nearest town it leads to (e.g. **CA** stands for Cadiz province). A blue panel with **A** (**autopista**) is for motorways. A green panel with **E** refers to the European numbering system.

M Madrid ring road
sur south

Driving in built-up areas

The navy on off-white sign at the entrance to a town or village gives you its name and sometimes the road number. It acts as a speed limit sign (normally 60 kilometres per hour or 35 mph). A similar sign with a red line through it ends the speed restriction.

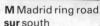

As you enter a town (**ciudad**) you often see signs with **en todo .. , en toda ..** (in the whole ..). They are reminders to keep to a certain speed limit, not to use the hooter, etc.

To get to the town centre follow **centro ciudad**. In smaller communities it may say **centro población**. A sign with **salida ciudad** shows you the way out of a town. If you want to avoid the centre altogether, look for roads marked **circunvalación** (bypass) or **vía de cintura** (ring road).

When you leave a town you're reminded by a blue on white sign to put on your seat belt (**cinturón de seguridad**).

Finding particular places (see also chapter 1)

To get to the airport look for **aeropuerto**. Once there **llegada(s)** takes you to arrivals, **salida(s)** to departures.

If a sign just says **puerto** or **pto**. it's a road leading to the harbour. Remember there are also a number of towns called **Puerto**.. (Port..).

Signs with **puerta** or **pta**. point to a town gate. **Puente** or **pte**. indicates a bridge. As you approach a river (**río**) there is often a white on reddish sign giving its name. If it's a small river it may say **arroyo**.

If you want to park watch out for **aparcamiento**, **parking** or **estacionamiento**.

A black on white direction sign with **viveros** doesn't lead to a town of that name but to a nursery selling plants!

Closed or restricted roads

If there's a diversion it will say **desvío**.

A road closed to traffic may have a sign **prohibido el paso** or there may be two red traffic lights (used in some towns to stop you driving up a one-way street in the wrong direction). The sign could also say **cortado**.

pesados heavy

23

A dead end will be marked **sin salida** (without exit). **Particular** warns you that the road is private, and as a rule only residents can use it.

Carril bus tells you it's a bus lane, **carril bici** a bicycle lane. **Carril cerrado** (in Catalonia **vía tancada**) indicates a lane closed to traffic.

ajenos not belonging
esta this
urbanización housing estate

On the open road

On main roads distance markers every kilometre or so show you how far away you are from a major town. This one with a red top tells you that you're on the Madrid trunk road 656 kilometres from the capital.

A continuous white line must not be crossed, so to make a U-turn or a left turn look for **cambio de sentido** (change of direction), sometimes without the symbol, sometimes just the symbol on its own.

Where you have to cross a railway line you'll see **paso a nivel** if it's a guarded level crossing, **paso sin guarda** if it's unguarded.

polígono industrial
industrial estate

Don't forget: **m** after a number means 'metres', not miles.

a 300 m
300 metres ahead

Where a road comes close to a railway line there's usually a sign telling you which line it is. It will say **ferrocarril** (railway) or **F.C.** for short (no connection with a football club!).

Things you should or shouldn't do

Remember that the word telling you what to do usually ends in **-ar, -a(n)** or **-e(n)**.

circular al paso ⎫
circule despacio ⎭ drive slowly
circulen amodiño (Galician) drive carefully
respete la señalización observe the signs

dejen libre el carril del autobús keep out of bus lane

no bloquear cruce don't block junction

recuerde remember (i.e. a reminder that a speed limit is in force)

Watch out for . . .

* **peligro, precaución, atención**: they warn you of hazards ahead
* **cambio de rasante** brow of a hill
* **carretera en mal estado** bad road surface
* **desprendimiento** falling stones
* **escalón lateral** verge below road level
* **entrada** or **salida de camiones** entrance or exit for lorries
* **obras** road works
* **travesía** crossing point for pedestrians

muchos niños
many children

en 2 kms for 2 kilometres
rogamos perdonen las molestias
sorry for the inconvenience

If you need help (see also 2c)

There are emergency phones on many main roads.
Some connect you to a motoring organisation like **ADA** (**Ayuda del Automovilista, ayuda** = help).
Look out for patrol cars with **Ayuda de Carretera** run by the **Guardia Civil**.

❓Test yourself

1 Identify these 'false friends':
autocar carro circulación circular coche conductor particular

2 What's the difference between (i) **cinturón de seguridad** – **vía de cintura** (ii) **pta. – pte. – pto.**?

3 Where will you get to if you follow these signs?

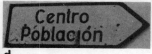

4 You want to get out of town.
Which sign points the way?

a

b

c

5 What are you asked to do?

a

b

c

d

6 What are you being warned about?

a

b

c

d

e

f

7 What's the difference between
these prohibition signs?

a

b

8 What do you make of these signs?

a

b

c

d

Can that be right?

b Finding somewhere to park

👤 Key words

aparcar
(to park)

aparcamiento, aparcadero car park

entrada
(way in)

estacionar
(to park)   *but*

estacionamiento (shortened to **estacio.**) parking
estación means station

hora(s)
(hour, o'clock)

shortened to **h, H, hrs., hras.**
horario times when parking restrictions are in force

salida
(exit, way out)

Names of different types of vehicle

Useful if you want to know whether a parking restriction applies to you or not.

Four-wheelers

autocares coaches *not* cars
camiones lorries
coches cars *not* coaches
but **coches de caballo** are
horsedrawn cabs
turismos private cars
vehículos ligeros light vehicles
vehículos pesados heavy vehicles

Two-wheelers

bicis = bicicletas bicycles
ciclomotores mopeds
motos = motocicletas motorbikes
vehículos de dos ruedas
two-wheelers

Street parking

alameda park
vieja old

* Look for the **P** symbol (white on blue or blue on white). Words on the sign often tell you
  - where you can park
  - how you should park, e.g. **en cordón**, **en línea**(in line) or **en batería** (side by side)
  - who can park: you can park your car if it says **coches**, **vehículos ligeros**, **turismos**. You can't park when you see **gran turismo** – that's for hire cars and coaches –, **coches S.P.** (**S.P.** = **servicio público**) for official cars and taxis, **camiones** for lorries, etc.

Beware the black **P** symbol on a white square inset on a 'no-waiting' sign: it allows parking only for certain vehicles or road users which may not include you, e.g. **motos** (motorbikes), **funcionarios** (officials), **usuarios Renfe** (railway station users).

* Look also for **estacionamiento**. Parking may be restricted to 30 minutes or 1 hour and to certain times of day. **Estacionamiento con horario limitado** or **zona (de) estacionamiento limitado** means it's limited stay parking. **Horario obligatorio** tells you when the restrictions apply. In most towns this is signposted with a 'no waiting' sign on a white background.

You may need a parking disc (**disco**) or card (**tarjeta** or **ticket**) which you normally buy from an **estanco** (tobacconist's). You mark the time of arrival and display the disc or card inside the windscreen (**parabrisas**).

Areas with similar parking restrictions are sometimes called **zona azul** (blue zone).

Parking is usually free during the long lunch hour.

* Watch out for 'no-waiting' signs that apply only on certain days, e.g. on market days (**días de mercado**), or at certain times – they mean you can park at all other times.

Parking may be prohibited in one half of the month, either **del 1 al 15** (from the 1st to 15th) or **del 16 al 31** or **del 16 a fin de mes** (end of the month). In the remainder of the month parking is allowed. But when a 'no-waiting' sign giving dates also says **tolerado** or **permitido** parking is permitted on those days.

* You may stop briefly when you see **parada momentánea** (**parada** = stop).

* Parking meters (**parquímetros**) of the 'pay and display' type are in use in many towns (see also p. 60, question 3). Look out for them when you see this sign:

Signs pointing to the ticket dispenser will say **expendedor tickets**.

hasta until

Don't park . . .

* where you see **aparcar** or **estacionar** coupled with **no**, **prohibido** or **no está permitido**

* where parking is private (**privado**) or reserved (**reservado**) for certain purposes or users

* where you see a 'no-waiting' sign with **ambos lados** (both sides) on it: it means 'no parking' on either side of the road

* where a '*no*-waiting' sign exempts certain road users which may not include you, e.g. **vecinos** (residents), **coches autorizados** (authorised vehicles)

* in front of exits or entrances for vehicles, particularly where it says **vado permanente** (in constant use)

profesores teaching staff

* where it says **carga y descarga** (loading and unloading), sometimes shortened to **C y D**

* where you see **grúa** (hoist) or **retirada** (removal) or both: you're being warned that your car will be towed away – no empty threat. You will have to pay a fine (**multa**) of several thousand pesetas and have to travel a fair way to recover your car.

* where the kerb is painted yellow or red and white

Off-street parking

* Look for **estacionamiento** or **estacio.**, **aparcamiento**, **aparcadero**, **parking** or the **P** symbol. **Vigilado** means there's an attendant (whom you tip), **gratuito** tells you it's free of charge.

Vigalpe name

* Most multistorey car parks are underground. Before driving in check whether it says **libre** (spaces) or **completo** (full).

At a barrier near the entrance you'll probably be asked to take (**recoja** or **tome**) a ticket. On the ticket machine it may say **tickets aquí** (tickets here). Ignore any machine with **abonados** – that's for season ticket holders.

Aviasa name

su your

To get into the car park on foot enter where it says **peatones** (pedestrians). To find the right level look for **planta**.

As a rule you pay before collecting your car, usually at a cash desk (**caja**).

To find your way out of the car park follow the sign **salida**.

pase por go to   **retirar** to remove
antes de before

② Test yourself

1 Identify these 'false friends':
autocares   coches   motos   planta   retirar   turismo

2 Where do these signs direct you to?

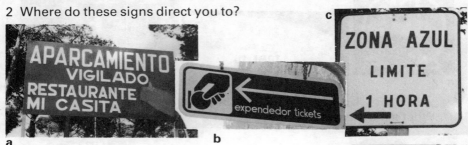

a

b

c

3 You're driving the family car. Can you park here?

a

b

c

d

4 Who can park here?

a

b

c

5 When can you park here?

a

b

c

d

6 You may come across these signs in a multistorey car park. What do they tell you?

a

b

c

d

7 What's the message on these signs?

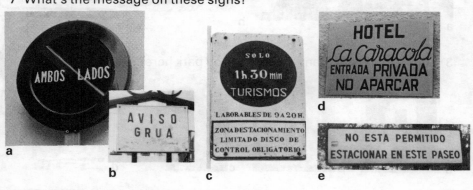

a

b

c

d

e

Can that be right?

No wonder the patio's inferior — they park on it!

c Motorway driving

🔒 Key words

autopista
(motorway)

but **autovía** is a dual carriageway

peaje
(toll)

importe de peaje toll charge – nothing to do with import

salida
(exit)

Joining the motorway

Look for **autopista** or the white on blue motorway symbol. Some signs also have **A** and the motorway number on them, and often name the places they lead to. Other white on blue signs with **A** and a number on them may be part motorway, part dual carriageway (**autovía**).

You have to pay a toll (**peaje**) on most stretches of motorway, even if there is no mention of it on the direction sign. In Catalonia it appears as **peatge**. Dual carriageways are toll free.

Paying the toll charge

Toll systems differ. On most motorways you're told to take a ticket (**recoja billete**) as you go on or at a barrier, and you pay at the exit. On others you pay before you use the motorway. The amount (**importe**) often depends on the cubic capacity of your vehicle. As you approach the barrier you're asked to have the toll charge ready (**preparar el importe de peaje**).

menos de under
más de over

Other motorway signs

If you want to rest or eat look for **área de descanso** (rest area) or **área de servicio** (service area). Some have limited opening times (**horario limitado**), others are permanently open (**servicio permanente**), though the sign is no guarantee that this is so! Many have picnic areas or a small self-service restaurant.

If you need petrol look for the petrol pump symbol or **gasolina** (petrol).

At regular intervals along the motorway there are white on blue signs showing how far away you are from the beginning or end of the **autopista**. This sign on the Seville-Cadiz motorway tells you that you are 80 kilometres from Seville.

If you want to leave the motorway

Exits are numbered and list the towns they lead to. They are signposted several kilometres ahead. There may be several exits to one town, sometimes identified as **norte** or **N** (north), **sur** or **S** (south), etc. In Catalonia an exit is called **sortida**.

At the entrance to some motorways there is a series of signs with **salida** showing you the number of the exit for each town along the route.

If you break down

There is a white and orange emergency phone every 2 kilometres. This connects you with the **servicio de autopista**. On this particular phone you press the button at the back marked **avería mecánica** if you need breakdown assistance. For medical help press **auxilio sanitario**.

A sign with **guardia civil** directs you to the motorway police.

destacamento unit

❷ Test yourself

1 What information do these signs provide?

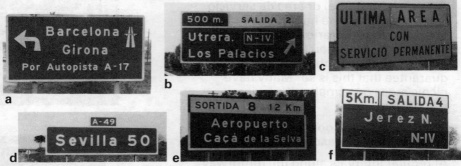

a

b

c

d

e

f

2 You're approaching the toll barrier. What are you asked to do?

a

b

3 You're approaching the frontier. What would you expect **aduana** to mean?

4 Which button do you press on the emergency phone if the car breaks down?

d Going to a service station

🔘 Key words

auto (car)	**automóvil** motor car *but* **auto escuela** driving school **autoservicio** is a self-service shop
cambio (change)	**cambio de aceite** oil change **recambios** spare parts
gasolina (petrol)	**gasolinera** petrol station **gasóleo, gas-oil** diesel
motor (engine)	*not* a motor car
servicio (service, servicing)	**estación (de) servicio** service station *but* **servicios** usually means toilets (see chapter 12)

Finding a service station

A sign pointing to one may say **gasolina**, **gasolinera**, **estación (de) servicio** or it may show the pump symbol.

A service station will often display a notice telling you when it's open (**abierto**) or closed (**cerrado**). The majority are open weekdays from 8 am to 8 pm or later but many close on Sunday afternoons. Some, like this one, are open day (**día**) and night (**noche**).

Andraitx
place name

SEAT car manufacturers
talleres workshops

When a service station is closed look for a notice telling you where to find the nearest ones (**más próximas**): it will give the road number (see p. 22), the number of the milestone closest to the next service station and the distance you have to travel.

All service stations are licensed and must display the licence number.

(see p. 22)

a...kms. ...kms from here

Filling up the tank

Grades of petrol are given in octane numbers (**NO** = **número de octanos** or **IO** = **índice de octanos**). There are two grades: **super**, shown on pumps as **gasolina 97**, roughly equivalent to four-star, and **normal** – **gasolina 92** – about the same as two-star. **Sin plomo** is unleaded.

Pumps marked **gasóleo** or **gas-oil** are for diesel – **gasóleo auto** or **gasóleo A** is for cars, **gasóleo B** for heavy vehicles. If you see **mezcla** (mixture) on a pump it's a two-stroke mixture.

There are as yet no brands. The name you see on many service stations and pumps is that of the company owning them, e.g. **CAMPSA**, **CEPSA** and **REPSOL**.

Normally you buy petrol in units of 100 pesetas unless you want to fill the tank right up (**lleno**). The price per litre (**precio por litro**) is the same throughout Spain.

Signs with **no fumar** (nothing to do with fumes) tell you not to smoke. This sign asks you to switch off (**apaguen**) the engine (**motor**).

Oil, air, water

If you need oil look for signs with **aceite**. For an oil change it will say **cambio de aceite**.

If the tyre pressures need checking look for **aire**. For water look for **agua**.

At many service stations you can buy ice cubes to keep your picnic cool or to take home. Look for **hielo** (ice) (see also picture on p. 81).

Getting the car washed or serviced

Lavado tells you that you can get your car washed. **Lavado automático** is a car wash.

Servicio or **servicios generales** advertise servicing. **Engrase** means 'lubrication', **puesto a punto** 'engine tuning'.

Getting the car repaired

Look for **servicio**, **garage** (or **garaje**), **taller** (or **talleres**). They may advertise **reparaciones** (repairs), **mecánica** (mechanical repairs), **electricidad** (electrical repairs), **carrocería** (coachwork), etc.

Ruiz Vera name

Many garages display their official rating which tells you what type of work they are licensed to do: here grade III is for general mechanical work only. The top rating of I means they can carry out electrical repairs and coachwork as well.

To get spare parts follow the signs **recambios** or **repuestos**.

If you have a puncture (**pinchazo**) watch out for signs with **neumáticos** (tyres), **servicio de neumáticos** or **pinchazos**.

❷ Test yourself

1 Identify these 'false friends': **motor   normal   reparaciones   super**

2 When would you be glad to see these signs?

a

b

d

c

3 You want to fill up with unleaded petrol. At which pump would you stop?

a

d

b

c

e

f

g

4 It's midnight and you're low on petrol.
   Where can you fill up?

5 The ignition is giving trouble. Which are the likeliest places to help?

6 What services are advertised here?

Can that be right?

3 Local transport

(see also chapter 4)

👤 Key words

billete (ticket)

correspondencia
(connection, interchange)

estación
(stop, station)

estación (de) autobuses, estación bus
bus or coach station

línea
(line, number, route)

línia (in Catalonia)

parada
(stop)

parada de autobuses bus stop
parada de taxi taxi rank

salida
(exit, departure)

salida de socorro emergency exit

viajeros (passengers)

a Going by bus

Different types of bus

A bus is called **autobús** or **bus**,
sometimes **ómnibus**. **Microbús** is a small
single-decker bus. A coach is **autocar**
but never **coche** – that's a car.

Bus services between major towns are often run by more than
one company, each with its own bus station (**estación de autobuses**).

Bus stops

These may be marked **parada**

Transportes La Unión name of company
S.A. = Sociedad Anónima Co. Ltd

— or they may show the bus number
(**línea**) with details of the route

— or they may have a black **P** on a white
square inset on a 'no waiting' sign
with the word **bus** – it means buses
only are allowed to stop or park there.

cabecera starting point

The destination or route is sometimes shown on the front or side of the bus. It may say **línea** or **L** before the bus number and the routing, or just give the bus number.

pza = **plaza** square

Buying a ticket

Local transport systems vary. In many towns you can get your ticket (**billete** or **ticket**) not only on the bus but also from special kiosks in the town centre and often from newsagents. The wording on the kiosk may be the name of the local transport company or it may alert you to a saving in fares.

venta sale

You can save money by buying tickets in batches or strips, sometimes advertised as **bonobus** (**bono** = voucher).

Getting on or off

You normally board the bus by the front door (**puerta delantera**) which may be marked **entrada** (entrance). You're not supposed to get on (**subir**) by the door at the back or in the centre – that's the exit (**salida**).

agente único one-man operated

b Taking a taxi

Taxi ranks

Signs will say **taxis, parada de taxi, P taxis**, or you'll see the white on blue **T** symbol which looks deceptively like a 'no through road' sign.

A taxi that's available will display a notice on the windscreen with **libre** (free) and show a green light at the top or side – otherwise it will say **ocupado**.

A sign **tele-taxi** or **radio-taxi** means that you can book the cab by phone.

In some tourist areas you have the chance to travel at a more leisurely pace by horsedrawn cab (**coche de caballo**).

c Using the underground

Getting a ticket

There are underground systems in
Madrid, Barcelona and Valencia.

To find an underground station look for
metro.

You can buy your ticket at the ticket
office (**taquilla**) or from machines
marked **billetes**. Where you see **precio
exacto** on a machine you need to put in
the exact fare. Slots marked **sencillo** are
for single tickets, **ida y vuelta** for returns.
If it says **devuelve cambio** it will give
change along with the ticket. You collect
your change from the slot marked
devolución moneda (**devolución** =
return, **moneda** = small change).

To get to the platform you may have to
operate a turnstile with your ticket: you
put it into the machine (**máquina**) where
it says **introduzca su billete** – provided
there isn't a sign like this!

fuera de out of

If you've bought a batch of tickets –
usually cheaper – you go through the
entrance marked **viajeros con billete**.

Travelling in the right direction

Metro lines are numbered and identified
by the name of the station at the end of
the line. Look for **línea** (**línia** in
Barcelona) or **dirección** and a place
name. Sometimes the platform (**vía**) and
a list of the stops (**estaciones**) along the
line are given. Many **metro** stations are
named after a city, a famous person, a
square, building or street.

If you have to change trains follow the
sign **correspondencia**.

ramal branch line

❷Test yourself

1 Identify these 'false friends':
   agente único   correspondencia   parada   vía

2 You're travelling by **metro**. Where do these signs direct you to?

a

b

c

3 You want to buy a ticket. Is either of these signs helpful?

a

b

4 Where should you board the bus? Where the door is open or closed?

a

b

5 What type of transport would you expect to find here?

a

b

c

d

Can that be right?

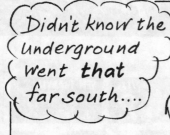

Didn't know the underground went *that* far south....

4 Going by train
(see also chapter 3)

Key words

billete (ticket)

estación (station)

ferrocarril (railway)

llegada (arrival)

salida (exit, departure)

vía (platform, track)

despacho de billetes ticket office

estación (de) ferrocarril railway station
jefe (de) estación station master

often shortened to **F.C.**, or **FF.CC.** for **ferrocarriles**

Getting to the station

Look for **estación** or **est.**, **estación (de) ferrocarril** or for **RENFE** (= **Red Nacional de Ferrocarriles Españoles** National Network of Spanish Railways).

The sign **ferrocarril** or **F.C.** usually tells you that you're close to or passing over a railway line – it's not intended to help you find the station!

Pto. = **Puerto** Port   **Sta.** = **Santa** Saint

Different types of train

The **Talgo** and the more modern **Talgo Pendular** are fast long-distance luxury trains. Other long-distance trains are the **Rápido**, **TER** (**Tren Eléctrico Rápido**) and **Electrotrén** (or **ELT**). **Expreso** is a night train with motorail service (**Auto Expreso**), *but* **Automotor** is a railcar.

Tranvía is a local electric train. **Semi-directo** or **sem.** tells you that the train stops at only a few stations. Some of these are called **interurbano**.

44

Individual carriages of long-distance trains may be marked **coche** with a number. If you're travelling by sleeper – you can only do this on a **Talgo** or **Expreso** – make for **camas** (beds) or **coche camas**. If you've booked a couchette look for **literas**. A buffet car will be marked **cafetería**.

Finding out about train times

The timetable may say **horario**. The one for departures will be headed **salidas** or **salidas de trenes**. An indicator board with **próxima(s) salida(s)** shows you which trains are about to leave. **Destino** tells you where they're going to, **tren** gives the type of train, **vía** is the platform (nothing to do with the route).

The arrivals board will say **llegadas** or **llegadas de trenes**. If you're meeting a train see if there's a notice board with **próximas llegadas** and **procedencia** (from).

Buying a ticket

At the station go to the counter marked **billetes**, **despacho de billetes**, **venta** (sale) **de billetes** or one which says **taquilla(s)** (ticket office(s)).

There may be separate counters for advance bookings (**venta anticipada**), for immediate travel (**salida inmediata**) and local and suburban travel (**cercanías**). **Largo recorrido** means it's for long-distance travel.

You can also buy train tickets at travel agencies and, in large towns, at **Renfe** offices. Your attention is often drawn to the fact that tickets are available on the spot (**en el acto**).

See if there's a leaflet or list of **días azules** (blue days). On many services there's a substantial discount on return tickets if you travel on a 'blue day'.

reserva electrónica computerised booking system

Finding the platform

Follow the sign **andén** or **andenes** (platforms), or **viajeros** (passengers) **con billete**. The individual platform will be shown as **vía** (track). On big stations you can generally check train details on the platform.

Use the subway when you see this:

Facilities at stations

Vestíbulo indicates the station hall. **Sala de espera** is a waiting room.

If you want a meal or drink and there's no **restaurante**, **cafetería** or **bar** look for **fonda** (inn) or **cantina** – *not* a canteen but a modest station buffet serving mainly drinks.

For registered luggage follow the sign **equipajes** or **facturación**.

At main line stations you'll also find **librerías** (bookstalls *not* libraries) and sometimes an **estanco** (kiosk selling stamps, cigarettes, tobacco, postcards, etc.).

❷ Test yourself

1 Identify these 'false friends':
   cantina   coche   despacho   largo   librería   venta   vía

2 You want to catch the next train from Barcelona to Paris. Which is the right ticket counter?

3 This train has everything. Say what facilities it offers.

4 What sort of information does
   this indicator board provide?

TREN	PROCEDENCIA	LLEGADA	VIA
EXPRESO	LEON	6.45	
ATLANTICO-EXPRESO	EL FERROL - LA CORUÑA	7.55	
EXPRESO	VIGO-PONTEVEDRA	8.15	
RIAS BAJAS EXPRESO	VIGO	8.50	
RIAS ALTAS EXPRESO	LA CORUÑA		
TER	FTES. ONORO - SALAMANCA	11.13.4	
SEMIDIRECTO	SALAMANCA	1.30.1	
TER	VIGO -	11.8.50	

5 Where do these signs point to?

a

b

c

6 Which are the right signs if you want to   (i) get your ticket   (ii) buy a
   guidebook   (iii) get some cigarettes   (iv) get some refreshments
   (v) sit down and have a rest?

a

b

c

d

e

7 You're rushing to catch a train.
   Is this sign any help?

Can that be right?

5 Somewhere to stay

👤Key words

acampar (to camp)	**acampados**, **campistas** campers **campamento**, **camping** campsite
	but **campo** means field or countryside, **campo de deportes** is a sports ground
alquilar (to let, rent)	**alquila(n)se**, **se alquila(n)** 'to let'
camas (beds)	
habitaciones (rooms)	
hospedaje (accommodation)	
hostal (modest hotel)	*not* a hostel – that's **albergue** **hostería** inn
huéspedes (guests)	**casa de huéspedes** guest house
piso (flat)	*but* shown with a number it means 'floor', 'storey'

Finding accommodation

If you want help with finding somewhere
to stay look for the official tourist office
(see also p. 61). They can give you all the
necessary information, but do not make
bookings. For that you need to go to an
agencia de viajes (travel agency).

Looking for a hotel

* **H** on a sign points the way to a hotel.
  They are graded one to five stars. You
  usually find a white on blue **H** on the
  outside of a hotel showing the requisite
  number of stars (see top of page).

Los Cigarrales
name of hotel

* A **hostal** (symbol **Hs**) offers more
  modest hotel-type accommodation.
  Their star rating is from one to three.
  They often occupy part of another
  building or perhaps just one floor
  (**piso**) (see also p. 17).

* A **hotel residencia** (**HR**) and a **hostal residencia** (**HsR**) are generally hotels without a restaurant other than perhaps a cafeteria.

* A **parador** is a state-run three to four-star hotel, with the symbol **A**. **Paradores** are often buildings of historic interest in attractive settings. They offer good accommodation, but you can stay for a few days only.

* **Albergues** are generally state-run roadside inns, more modest than a **parador**, *but* **albergues para jóvenes** are youth hostels.

* **Hosterías** are basically eating places although some offer accommodation.

Looking for simple accommodation

Look for a **pensión** (**P**) (boarding house). A **casa de huéspedes** (**CH**) (guest house) or a **fonda** (**F**) (modest inn) also offer basic accommodation but these two categories are being phased out though many of their signs are still in evidence. Other signs advertising accommodation may say **hospedaje** (lodging), **hay habitaciones** (rooms available) or **hay camas** (beds available).

Amenities you may be offered

Rooms may be advertised with bath (**baño**) or shower (**ducha**). Other attractions mentioned include **comidas** (meals), **comedor** (dining room), **jardín** (garden), **piscina** (swimming pool).

portero
caretaker

Self-catering accommodation

'To let' signs will say **se alquila(n)** or **alquíla(n)se** and will usually advertise **habitaciones** (rooms) or **piso** (flat). **Piso amueblado** means it's furnished. A sign with **razón** (enquiries) shows you where to get more details.

If you want a flatlet with service look for **apartamentos** (symbol **AT**). These are graded like hotels and rate between one and four 'keys'.

Camping

To find your way to a campsite look for **campamento** or **camping**.

Campsites are graded into three categories (**categorías**). Charges and often amenities, such as hot water (**agua caliente**), are displayed at or near the entrance (**entrada**).

Look at the entrance also for closing times, and for notices forbidding non-campers (**no acampados**, **no campistas**) or their cars (**coches**) to enter. These notices usually start with **prohibido el paso** (no entry).

cierre closing
a partir de from

Similar notices tell you until what time of night (**noche**) you're allowed to drive into the campsite.

ajenos not belonging

When you want to book in, make for **recepción**.

Washing facilities may be signposted **aseos**. Women look for **señoras** or **S**, men for **caballeros** or **C**. For hot water the sign will say **caliente**, for cold it will say **fría**.

Places for washing up may be labelled **fregadero** (kitchen sink) or **vajilla** (crockery). Wash your laundry where you see **ropa** (clothes) or **lavadero** (laundry room). If you need drinking water look for **agua potable** or just **potable**. Leave any rubbish where it says **basura**. A door marked **botiquín** means there's a first aid kit or room (see also p. 89).

❷ Test yourself

1 Identify these 'false friends':
   habitación   hostal   pensión

2 What's the difference between **campamento** and **campo**?

3 What kind of accommodation is offered here?

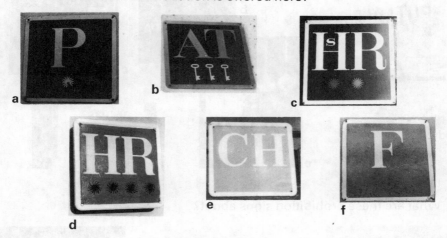

a   b   c   d   e   f

4 What's the difference between these two adverts?

a   b

5 What amenities do these places advertise?

a   b   c   d   e

6 These signs are on a campsite. What do they mark?

a Lavadero Fregadero →

b SOLO ROPA

c CALIENTE

d POTABLE

e SOLO VAJILLAS

f DUCHAS CABALLEROS

7 What are these prohibition signs about?

a PROHIBIDO PASAR COCHES A PARTIR DE LAS 12 DE LA NOCHE

b ¡ATENCION! PROHIBIDO EL PASO A LOS NO CAMPISTAS INFORMESE EN RECEPCION
SILENCIO ~ NO TRAFICO DE 12'30 A 7'30

c PROHIBIDO EL PASO A TODA PERSONA AJENA A ESTE CAMPING 15

Can that be right?

What? No naughty weekends?

SOLO CAMPING. →

52

6 Using the post office and telephones

Key words

cartas
(letters)

correos   **lista de correos** 'poste restante'
(post office)

monedas (coins)

sellos (stamps)

a Going to the post office

This is the post office symbol. The post
office colours are yellow and red.

Post office facilities

Where you see **correos y telégrafos** you
can also send cables and telegrams – but
you cannot make phone calls (see p. 55).
The sign **caja postal** means that there is
a post office savings bank. This may be
housed in the post office or a separate
building. It's the place where you can
cash Girobank postcheques (see also
p. 58).
In very small communities the post office
may be combined with other services!

Opening hours

Post offices are generally open on
weekdays (**laborables**) from 9 am till
2 pm, on Saturdays until 1 pm. Some of
the bigger ones are also open in the late
afternoon, but there are many local and
seasonal variations. To check look for
horario (opening hours).

In big cities post offices stay open
throughout the day till 8 pm or 9 pm for
certain services, such as telegrams and
the sale of stamps. For a round-the-clock
telegram service the notice will say
servicio permanente.

HORARIO
laborables:9a 12

Buying stamps

Look for the signs **venta de sellos** (sale of stamps) or just **sellos**. Stamp collectors should make for the counter **sellos para colecciones**.

You can also buy stamps at a tobacconist's shop or kiosk (**estanco**). You recognise them by the reddish brown and yellow sign with the **T** symbol and **tabacos** (tobacco and cigarettes). They are open during shopping hours.

Different post office counters

If you want to register your mail go to the counter **certificados**. There may be separate counters for inland mail (**para España**) and for abroad (**extranjero**). For airmail it will say **avión** (short for **por avión**, by plane), for special delivery **urgentes**. To collect 'poste restante' items make for **lista de correos**.

Counters for posting parcels are marked **admisión de paquetes**, the one for collecting parcels will say **entrega** (delivery) **de paquetes**.

Posting your mail

A letterbox (**buzón**) is yellow with red bands and says **cartas** (letters). Where collection times are given – and this isn't always the case – look under the heading **horas de recogida** (for days of the week see p. 13).

Red letterboxes with yellow bands are for special delivery mail (**correo urgente**). You can use it for inland mail or for abroad by paying a surcharge. There are collections even on Saturday and Sunday afternoons.

Outside big post offices there are often separate slots for different types of mail, e.g. **avión**, **extranjero**, **impresos** (printed matter), **urgentes**.

Don't be fooled by letterboxes with **cartas** or **buzón** on doors and walls of banks and other businesses – they're only meant for mail to those premises.

b Making phone calls

The telephone service is run by the **Compañía Telefónica Nacional de España**, commonly called **la telefónica**.

Using a public phone box

You can make any kind of call (**llamada** or **conferencia**) whether it is local (**urbano**), national (**interurbano**) or international (**internacional**) from coin-operated phone boxes in the street. They are bright blue.

Calls are timed. The minimum charge for a local call – cheaper after 8 pm – is 10 pesetas, i.e. you need two five-peseta coins. For long-distance and international calls – cheaper between 10 pm and 8 am – have a good supply of 25 and 100 peseta coins ready. Place (**deposite** or **coloque**) plenty of coins (**monedas**) in the sloping groove (**ranura**) on top of the phone – you need to be tall to see it! Dial. The coins will drop in as you use up the units. Replenish as necessary.

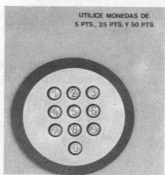

utilice use

Phoning from a *telefónica*

In most large towns there's a **telefónica** office with rows of booths where you can make phone calls. It operates on weekdays from 9 am till lunchtime and again in the late afternoon and evening. For local calls there are coin-operated phones. For other calls you may be allocated a **cabina** (phone booth). You dial the number yourself and pay at the counter when you've finished.

In tourist areas small temporary **telefónicas** appear during the season. Look for a silver grey prefab with a blue band at the top. These temporary **telefónicas** stay open late, some till 10 or 11 pm. Similar telephone facilities may be signposted **sala de teléfono**, **servicios telefónicos** or **locutorio**. For opening hours, look under **horario**, sometimes **horario del locutorio**. Calls from a **telefónica** or a public phone box will be cheaper than from a hotel.

Emergency calls (see p. 93).

❷ Test yourself

1. Identify these 'false friends':
   cabina   cartas   certificados   conferencia

2. At which of these would you get stamps for your mail?

a

b

c

3. You want to send your mail back home. Which is the correct slot?

4. You want to send a parcel abroad. Which counter is right?

a

b

c

56

5 What services would you expect to find at these post offices?

a

b

6 You want to make a phone call from Malaga to Madrid. What instructions are you given?

UTILICE MONEDAS DE:

5 ptas. para llamadas **Urbanas**
25 ptas. para llamadas **Interurbanas y Nacionales**
100 ptas. para llamadas **Internacionales**

7 On what days can you phone from here?

HORARIO DEL LOCUTORIO
DIAS LABORABLES
9 A 13 Y 17 A 21
DOMINGOS Y FESTIVOS
CERRADO

Can that be right?

But this letterbox is for cards only, dear!

7 Coping with money

👤 Key words

billete
(bank note)

caja
(cash desk,
cashier's, checkout)

cambio
(change, exchange,
exchange rate)

moneda
(coin, currency)

(horario de) caja banking hours
caja (de) ahorros savings bank
cajero automático cash dispenser

cambio de divisas, cambio de moneda
currency exchange
oficina de cambio exchange bureau

Where you can change money

At almost any bank (**banco**, occasionally **banca**). There are over 50 banking groups in Spain.

Don't be misled by **Banco Vitalicio** – that's an assurance company, or by **Banco Hipotecario** – that's a building society. **Autobanco** is the sign for a drive-in bank, though in practice they're rarely in operation and are used instead as a bank's car park!

You can change money at the bigger branches of a savings bank (**caja de ahorros**). Similar banks called **caja** may also offer exchange facilities, for instance some branches of a **Caja Rural**. In most towns and holiday resorts the **Caja Postal** (short for **Caja Postal de Ahorros**, post office savings bank) will encash Girobank postcheques and will change travellers cheques and foreign currency into pesetas (see also p. 53). They also accept Visa cards up to a limited amount.

You can change money at airports, at some travel agencies (**agencias de viajes**) and at exchange bureaux. Look for **oficina de cambio**, **cambio de divisas**, **cambio de moneda** or just **cambio**.

Changing money at a bank

Counters may say **cambio** or **divisas**, but more often than not there's no sign at all. At the end of the transaction you generally collect your money from the cashier where you see **caja**.

If you have a bank cash card which you can use to get pesetas at a bank in Spain look for **cajero automático** (cash dispenser) or a cashpoint operated by **Telebanco 4B** or **ServiRed**.

 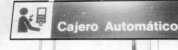

esta oficina this office

Banking hours

Banking hours vary. Many banks are open from 8.30 or 9 am till 4 or 4.30 pm Mondays to Thursdays, till 2 pm on Fridays, and – except in summer – on Saturdays and on the eve of public holidays (**vísperas de fiestas**) till about 1 pm. Watch out for local and seasonal variations. To check on opening hours look for **horario de caja**. Exchange bureaux at travel agencies and elsewhere usually operate during shopping hours (see p. 76).

Horario de Caja

Lunes a Jueves de 8,30 - 16,30 h.

Viernes de 8,30 - 14 h.

Sabado de 8,30 - 13 h.

Coping with coin-operated machines

On parking meters and other machines, you must use coins (**monedas**) and not a credit card where it says **pago en metálico** (payment in cash).

You may be told what coins the machine takes (**admite**) or be asked to put in coins (**introducir monedas**). Make sure you put in the exact money where it says **precio exacto** or **no devuelve cambio** (no change given).

The notice in the picture is on an automatic photo booth.

❷ Test yourself

1 At which of these are you likely to be able to change travellers cheques?

a OFICINA DE CAMBIO

b

BILLETES	
COMPRA	VENTA
121.90	126.55
99.79	103.54
18.97	19.68
204.48	212.15
76.25	79.11
304.11	315.52
64.52	66.94
8.66	8.99
57.23	59.38
18.84	19.55
16.82	17.45
17.52	18.18
173.04	179.52
917.60	952.01

c BANCO HIPOTECARIO D ESPAÑA

d CAJA AHORROS RONDA

2 What does it say here about opening hours?

a HORARIO AL PUBLICO
16 DE SEPTIEMBRE al
19 DE JUNIO
LUNES A JUEVES : DE 8.30 a 16.30 hrs
VIERNES : DE 8.30 a 14 "
SABADOS : DE 8.30 a 13 "

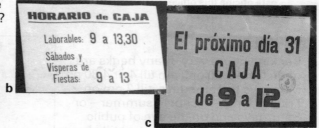

b HORARIO de CAJA
Laborables: 9 a 13,30
Sábados y Vísperas de Fiestas: 9 a 13

c El próximo día 31 CAJA de 9 a 12

3 This parking meter tells you to put in coins until you obtain the required parking time. Does it give change?

PAGO EN METALICO

1 Introduzca las monedas hasta obtener el tiempo de estacionamiento deseado. (NO DEVUELVE CAMBIO)

Can that be right?

A "safe" place to leave my car?

autobanco

8 Sightseeing

👤 Key words

ayuntamiento
(town hall,
town council)

casa
(house)

casa consistorial
city hall

castillo
(castle)

exposición
(exhibition)

sala de exposiciones exhibition room or hall

hora
(hour, o'clock)

horas de visita, horario opening times

iglesia
(church)

iglesia parroquial parish church

real
(royal)

real academia royal academy
palacios reales royal palaces

turismo
(tourism)

but

oficina de turismo tourist office
turismos are private cars

viaje
(trip, journey)

Important words

entrada way in, admission fee
salida way out
subida way up

Finding out what there is to see

You can get brochures, maps, etc. from
the official tourist offices. Signs may say
**oficina de turismo, oficina de
información y turismo, delegación
provincial de turismo, patronato
municipal de turismo**.

excmo. = excelentísimo
the most excellent
patronato board

Seeing the sights

To book an **excursión** go to an **agencia
de viajes** (travel agents).

A sightseeing tour around town is a
visita. If it's a guided tour it's called
visita con guía (with a guide). In many
places you can hire a **guía** at official
rates, but more often than not a guide

comes up to you unofficially to take you around (tip, **propina**, expected).

Santa Cruz Holy Cross

If you want to explore by yourself it may be worth looking for signs with **murallas** (ramparts), **recinto amurallado** (walled part of town), **puerta** (city gate), **puerto** (harbour, port), **casa** (often a house of historic interest or a museum), **vista panorámica** (panoramic view), **barrio** (usually an old quarter of special interest like the **barrio de Santa Cruz** in Seville). **Viejo** or **vieja** means something is old. A Roman numeral after **siglo** or **S.** (century) tells you roughly when a place was built.

frente opposite

Watch out for this symbol:
It pinpoints places of special interest, e.g. **monumento histórico** (historic building or site), **cueva** (cave), **ermita** (hermitage).

Visiting churches

Look for **catedral**, **iglesia** (church), **iglesia parroquial** or **parroquia** (parish church), **capilla** (chapel).

Santo Domingo St Dominic

Famous churches are often signposted with just their name. This starts as a rule with **San** (**S.**), **Santo** (**Sto.**), **Santa** (**Sta.**) all meaning 'Saint', or with **Ntra. Sra.** = **Nuestra Señora** (Our Lady).

If you want to visit the cloisters follow the sign **claustro**.

El Greco Spanish painter
reyes monarchs
San Juan St John

. . . castles and palaces

Castles in Spain are **castillos**, although you'll also see **alcázar** which indicates a castle or palace often dating back to Moorish times. A sign with **alcazaba** directs you to a fortified hilltop citadel – though it may be in ruins.

Palacio is a palace or elegant town house, but occasionally it's no more than an impressive description of some official building like the **palacio de comunicaciones** (main post office in Madrid) or of a shop.

. . . museums and exhibitions

The name of a museum sometimes tells you what to expect – **museo** (or **casa**) **del Greco** (paintings by El Greco), **museo de bellas artes** (fine arts), **museo de arte románico** (Romanesque art).

mezquita mosque

Inside a museum the individual rooms are called **salas**. There may be notices telling you which way to go (**sentido de la visita**). If you want to visit an exhibition watch out for **exposición**.

pinturas paintings **paisajes** landscapes
bodegones still lifes

. . . parks and gardens

Jardín is a garden – **jardines** are usually castle grounds.

Parque is a park, **parque de atracciones** a fun fair *but* **parque de bomberos** is a fire station, **parque infantil** a children's playground.

Do's and don'ts when sightseeing

Most signs ask you to refrain from doing various things, and start with **no** or **prohibido**. Watch out for **fumar** (to smoke), **tocar** (to touch), **hacer fotos** (to take photographs). You may be asked to be appropriately dressed when visiting a church, or not to sit down (**no sentarse**) when you're in a museum.

traje de baño swimsuit
pantalón corto shorts

Some signs tell you politely that you're requested (**se ruega**) not to touch things. In open spaces you're urged to respect your surroundings and not to walk on (**no pise**) the grass (**césped**).

Times when places are open

Look for **horario** or **horas de visita**, or just a list of the days and times when you can visit. These are often divided into **mañana** (morning) or **tarde** (late afternoon).

no toquen
don't touch

Castilla Castile
paso libre free entry
coches cars

Many museums and castles are closed (**cerrado**) one day a week, and nearly all of them close for a long lunch break.

Times are often given **de** or **desde** (from), **a** or **hasta** (to, until). For the latest time of admission it may say **última visita**.

If you see this sign you're out of luck!

obras repairs

Getting a ticket

The ticket office will probably be marked **despacho de billetes** or just **billetes** (tickets), sometimes **taquilla**.

For the entrance fee look for **tarifa**, **entrada** or **precio** (price). When visits are free it will say **entrada libre**, **entrada gratuita** or **gratis**.

Exploring the countryside

Tourist routes of scenic, historic or other interest are signposted **ruta**.
Along the road there may be sights of historic or artistic interest.

pueblos blancos
white villages

As you approach a village or town there are often signs alerting you to what is worth visiting. But signs with **bienvenido** merely bid you welcome.

puente bridge

ciudad town

❷ Test yourself

1 Identify these 'false friends': **exposición**   **real**

2 Distinguish between these: (i) **Castilla – castillo** (ii) **sala – salida**

3 What sort of places would you expect to find if you followed these signs?

4 These signs are outside some buildings. What information do they provide?

Parroquia de Santa Catalina

Ayuntamiento

a

Castillo de Santiago (S. XV)

b

ALCAZAR DE LOS REYES CRISTIANOS (ULTIMA VISITA 1'45)

HORAS (MAÑANA 9'30 A 1'30

DE VISITA (TARDE 4 A 7

c

5 What would you expect to see if you entered these buildings?

MUSEO DE BELLAS ARTES

a

CAPILLA DE MONTSERRAT

b

6 You're spending the day visiting museums and old palaces. Where do these signs direct you to?

ENTRADA A LOS REALES ALCAZARES

a

SUBIDA A LA TORRE

b

SALIDA AL FONDO

c

7 What are you asked not to do?

PROHIBIDO HACER FOTOS

a

NO FUME GUARDE SILENCIO

b

POR FAVOR NO SENTARSE

c

NO PISE EL CESPED

d

8 These signs are on the outskirts of towns. What are they about?

BIENVENIDO A SANLUCAR DE BARRAMEDA

a

MOGUER

LE INVITA A VISITAR:
Convento de Sta. Clara
Convento de S. Francisco
Casa Museo de
Juan Ramón y Zenobia

b

Ruta del Vino
Puerto de Santa Maria

c

9 Enjoying yourself

🔑 Key words

baño
(bathing)

baño de sol sunbathing
bañarse to bathe

deporte
(sport)

campo de deportes sports ground
deportivo sports ...
puerto deportivo marina

ducha
(shower)

ducharse to take a shower

juego
(game)

jugar to play
juguetes toys

localidad
(seat, ticket)

despacho de localidades box office

piscina
(swimming pool)

playa
(beach)

platja (in Catalonia)

sala
(hall)

sala de fiestas dance hall
salón large hall

taquilla
(ticket office)

FIESTA SEVILLANA
entre gracia y salero...
SIRTAKIS
es el primero
CONCURSO DE FLAMENCO
Premios en metálico para los participantes
Viernes, día 22 de Abril SEMI FINAL
Sábado, día 23 de Abril GRAN FINAL

a Doing your own thing

Going swimming

If you want a swimming pool look for **piscina**. You may have to pay to go in. For the appropriate charges look under **adultos** and **niños** (children).
If you're keen on sea or river bathing look for **playa**.

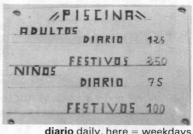

PISCINA
ADULTOS   DIARIO   125
           FESTIVOS   250
NIÑOS   DIARIO   75
           FESTIVOS   100

diario daily, here = weekdays

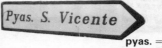

Pyas. S. Vicente

pyas. = **playas**
S. = **San** Saint

Beach huts are **casetas**. Sun shelters are advertised as **tiendas**, sun loungers as **tumbonas**.

Changing rooms are **vestuarios**, cubicles are **cabinas**. **Guardarropa** is the place for leaving your clothes.

subir to go up
calzado wearing shoes

ACCESO PROHIBIDO SUBIR CALZADO   VESTUARIOS

If you want the showers follow the sign **duchas**.

The section for women is marked **señoras** or **S**, the one for men **caballeros** or **C**.

On the beach watch out for signs warning you that bathing may be dangerous (**peligroso**) – red flag, or that you should take care (**precaución**) – orange flag. Bathing is safe where you see **buen estado del mar** (calm sea) or a green flag. It is forbidden where it says **prohibido bañarse**.

en el baño when bathing

Water sports

Sailboard enthusiasts look for **windsurf**! Water skiers should look for **esquí acuático**.

You may want to hire a boat (**embarcación**). Pedal boats are **embarcaciones a pedal**. If you enjoy rowing (**remar**) see if there are **embarcaciones a remo**. Canoes are **canoas**. If you want to hire a motorboat look for **motora**. Signs on boats with **paseo por el mar** advertise sea trips.

A sign **puerto deportivo** points the way to a marina.

CADE name of sports ground

Other sports

The local sports ground is signposted **campo de deportes**.

An area for sporting activities is called **zona deportiva** or **área deportiva**. You often find them in large parks and in residential areas.

La Espuela name of stables

Many sports clubs display signs informing you that admission is for members (**socios**) only.

Popular sports include **golf**, **tenis**, **equitación** (riding) and **tiro de pichón** (clay pigeon shooting). If you're interested in bowling watch out for **bolera** (bowling alley). **Bolera americana** tells you it's ten-pin bowling (**bolo** = pin).

b Entertainments

Spectator sports

Very popular are basketball (**baloncesto**)
and football (**fútbol**). Indoor football, i.e.
five-a-side, is **fútbol sala**. **Campeonato**
tells you that a championship match is
being played. There may be special
ticket offices in the street advertising the
sale of tickets (**venta de localidades**).
To find your way to the stadium look for
estadio.

patronato board   **mundial** world

Toros, short for **corrida de toros**, are
bullfights. They are mostly held in the
late afternoon on Sundays or public
holidays. Tickets are sold at the bullring
(**plaza de toros**) and at slightly higher
prices in many bars and cafés, and at
makeshift ticket offices in the street. The
cheaper tickets are in the sun (**sol**), the
more expensive ones in the shade
(**sombra**).

Dancing and other festivities

Salas de fiestas are for dancing.
Sometimes you can watch displays of
Spanish dancing there.

Places called **tablao** are known
for their authentic flamenco
dance shows.

A **fiesta** can be a party or other
festivity, often with dancing (**bailes**) and   **Los Gallos** name
singing (**canciones**).
This one is a little out of the ordinary:

Posters with **feria** tell you that a fair is
being held.

brujas witches

Going to a performance

Seats are **localidades**.
No hay warns you it's sold out.

zarzuela operetta

If you're going to the cinema and want to know what's on today look for **hoy**. **Hoy tarde** tells you it's on this afternoon or this evening. **Sesión contínua** means it's a continuous performance.

In many places seating is arranged according to even (**pares**) and odd (**impares**) numbers.

a partir de from

Other entertainments

Bingo is much in vogue. To be allowed in you need to show your passport. Spaniards must produce their **DNI = Documento Nacional de Identidad**.

Beware **casino**: it may be a casino but more commonly it's a men's club.

Amusement arcades may be signposted **juegos recreativos**, **sala de juego** or **salón recreativo**, but people under 18 (**menores**) are not supposed to go in.

With many places of entertainment you may be refused admission where it says **reservado el derecho de admisión**. There may be restrictions on the age of young people.

años years
mayores 'of age'

Something for the children

In the season there are many funfairs (**parques de atracciones**), each with its colourful merry-go-round (**carrusel**). You may be told to buy tokens (**saquen fichas**) or pay so much for each trip (**viaje**).

If you want a children's playground look for **parque infantil**. For a crèche it will say **guardería**.

cadenas chains, i.e. seats hanging on chains
Confran name

❷ Test yourself

1 Identify these 'false friends': **diario embarcación localidades playa**

2 This way to the bar.
  Where else?

3 You're in the swimming pool.

  (i) Where does this door lead to?

  (ii) What should
       or shouldn't
       you do?

a

b

4 You're going to the beach.
  What facilities are there?

5 You've been lazing about all morning.
  What's on offer here?

a

b

c

70

6 Your children want to go on the merry-go-round. What do you have to do?

7 What does it say here about admission?

a

b

8 You're going to an open air concert and have seats 19, 21, 23. Which sign should you follow?

a   b

9 What is the gist of this sign?

10 What does it say on these two signs?

a

b

Can that be right?

10 Shops and services

👤 Key words

abrir (to open)	**abrimos** we open **abierto** open (**obert** in Catalonia)
alimento (food)	**alimentación** food shop **alimentos de régimen** health food
autoservicio (self-service shop)	
caja (cash desk, checkout)	**caja rápida** express checkout
cerrar (to close)	**cerramos** we close **cerrado** closed (**tancat** in Catalonia)
mercado (market)	**hipermercado** superstore **supermercado** supermarket
precio (price)	
rebajas (reductions, 'sale')	**rebajado** reduced *but* **bajada** means 'way down' **planta baja** is the ground floor

Nuevo **SUPER MERCADO** DE ALIMENTACION
 PLANTA SOTANO El Corte Inglés
 PRECIADOS

Preciados name

Shop signs to look for

Most shops advertise their goods and
services prominently. Look for words
with ... **ería**:
    carnicería butcher's
    ferretería hardware shop
    papelería stationer's
    zapatería shoe shop, also shoemaker's

FERRETERIA PAPELERIA FOTOCOPIAS

Quite a few signs are guessable, e.g.
perfumería, but beware of some
misleading names:
    droguería sells household goods, toiletries, etc. *not* drugs
    librería bookshop, bookstall *not* a library – that's **biblioteca**

ZAPATERIA IGLESIAS

Iglesias name

You might see the names of the articles
you want to buy:
    calzados footwear
    confecciones ready-made clothes *not*
    confectionery – that's **confitería**
    juguetes toys
    libros books

CONFECCIONES

A sign with **casa** (house) often indicates a food or wine shop, or some specialist shop.

Autoservicio means it's self-service, nothing to do with cars.

If you want souvenirs or presents

Look for **recuerdos** (souvenirs *not* records – that's **discos**).
Gift shops advertise their wares with **regalos** (gifts) – **artículos (de) regalo**, **objetos (de) regalo** or **objetos para regalos** – but **regalo** on its own has a different meaning (see 'Spotting a bargain', p. 74). A local craft shop with the sign **artesanía** (handicrafts) may be a good place for buying presents.
If you want to buy flowers look for **flores**.

Miko
brand name

. . . cigarettes or tobacco

You can get these – at slightly lower cost – from an **estanco**. That's a shop or kiosk licensed to sell tobacco (**tabacos**) and cigarettes (**cigarrillos**) as well as stamps (**sellos**), tickets for parking, etc. They also have postcards (**postales**).
You recognise an **estanco** by the reddish brown and yellow **T** sign (see also p. 54).

. . .newspapers and books

For books look for **librería** or **libros**.
For newspapers watch out for signs with **prensa** (press), **periódicos** (newspapers) and **revistas** (magazines). You can also get them at some **papelerías** and of course at newsstands (**kioskos** or **quioscos**).

Shopping in department stores

The different departments carry signs similar to the ones you see on shops – they end in . . . **ería**, e.g. **bisutería** (fancy jewellery), **cristalería** (glassware), or they name the goods on display, e.g. **camisas** (shirts), **blusas** (blouses), **faldas** (skirts), **trajes** (dresses or suits), **tejidos** (fabrics).

Some stores have a self-service food department (**alimentación** or **supermercado**).

The different floors are marked **planta**: **planta baja** is the ground floor, **planta sótano** or just **sótano** is the basement, etc. (see also p. 17).

Spotting a bargain

Rebajas (reductions) tells you that there's a sale on. **Rebajas de verano** are summer sales, but a closing down sale is **liquidación**.

Reductions on certain goods are usually marked **descuento** (discount). Special offers may be labelled **oferta**. **Regalo** (gift) means it's a bargain.

Any mention of **precio** or **precios** should attract your attention, e.g. **precios interesantísimos** (very attractive prices, literally 'most interesting'). But where you see **precio fijo** it means that goods are sold at a fixed price and bargaining is out.

champú
shampoo

Supermarket shopping

Many self-service shops, however small, call themselves **supermercado** or have a sign **autoservicio**. The large out-of-town ones are called **hipermercado**.

Suau name

At the entrance to many supermarkets there are notices asking you to leave your shopping bag (**bolso** or **bolsa de compras**) or parcels (**paquetes**) at reception and to take a basket (**cesto**) or trolley (**carrito** or **carro**).

There are often notices asking you to serve yourself (**sírvase Vd. mismo**).

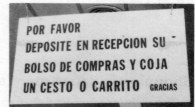

su your   **coja** take

The different sections are usually marked, e.g. **galletas** (biscuits), **conservas** (tinned food), **congelados** (frozen foods), **limpieza** (cleaning materials).

huevos eggs

You leave where it says **caja**. If you have only a few items (**artículos** or **unidades**) go to the **caja rápida**.

Markets and small food shops

You can buy a wide range of food, including dairy produce, meat, poultry, sausages, fish, in the local market (**mercado**).

These are usually covered markets, particularly in the hotter parts of Spain, and are held most weekday mornings.

limpieza cleanliness
comodidad convenience
más calidad better quality
menos dinero lower cost

There are also plenty of small food shops:

* for bread (**pan**) look for **panadería** (baker's); some also sell cakes and pastries (**pasteles**), but for a proper pastry shop watch out for **pastelería**, **repostería** or **confitería**

* for a general food shop the sign will say **alimentación**; if they sell mainly groceries it may say **ultramarinos**, **comestibles** or **colmado**

* for fruit (**fruta**) and vegetables (**verduras** or **hortalizas**) watch out for **frutería**; if it says **frutos secos** it's a shop selling dried fruit and nuts

* for health foods look for **alimentos de régimen**

* for fresh meat (**carne**) look for **carnicería** (butcher's); for cooked meats the sign will say **charcutería** though you will find that they also sell cheeses (**quesos**)

* for uncooked poultry look for **pollos** (chickens), but *not* **pollos asados** – that's roast chickens; poultry shops normally sell eggs (**huevos**) as well

pavos turkeys
doc. = **docena** dozen
primera first (grade)
segunda second (grade)
E = **extra** extra large

* for fresh fish (**pescado**) go to a **pescadería**; many also sell shellfish (**marisco**); if it's cooked shellfish you want look for **marisquería**

* for sweets find a **confitería** or **repostería**, or look for signs with **dulces** or **golosinas** (sweets), **caramelos** (wrapped sweets), **bombones** (chocolates), **mazapán** (marzipan)

* for wines look for **vinos** or find a **bodega** where you can buy wine from the barrel

cervezas beer

Getting things done

If you need something repaired look out for **reparación** or **reparaciones** (repairs). You can get shoes repaired at a **zapatería** or where you see this sign:

C.Lora name

If you want to go to the hairdresser's, you need to find a **peluquería**. Women look for **señoras** or **mujer** (woman), men for **caballeros** or **hombre** (man). A barber's is a **barbería**.

If you want something washed go to a **lavandería** (laundry). For dry-cleaning (**limpieza en seco**) go to a **tintorería**.

Signs in shop windows with **se** ... alert you to services such as key cutting (**se hacen llaves** = keys cut), film developing (**se revelan fotos** = films developed), or 'zip fitting' (**se colocan cremalleras** = zips fitted).

Shopping hours

Opening hours (**horario**) vary according to season and region. As a rule shops

invierno winter, i.e. from about October

open around 8 or 9 am, have a long lunch break – they may reopen as late as 5 pm – and stay open until 8 pm or 8.30 pm. Many shops close on Saturday afternoon (**sábado tarde**). A handful of food shops are open on Sunday mornings.

Shops that stay open all day advertise this with **horario continuado** or **abierto a mediodía** (open midday, i.e. lunchtime).

❓Test yourself

1 Identify these 'false friends':
autoservicio cigarrillos comodidad confecciones droguería librería planta recuerdos reparaciones

2 Can you buy groceries at all these shops?

a

b

c

3 What can you buy here?

a

b

4 What would make you stop here?

a

b

c

5 You're hunting for souvenirs and presents.
Why might these signs attract you?

a

b

c

6 What's being advertised for
men and what for women?

a

b

7 You're in a self-service shop.
What do these signs say?

a SIRVASE VD. MISMO *gracias*

b LIMPIEZA

c CAJA RAPIDA MAXIMO 10 UNIDADES

d
NO SE PERMITE LA ENTRADA CON BOLSOS O PAQUETES GRANDES

8 You want to have your hair done.
Which is the right sign?

a TINTORERIA

b PELUQUERIA DE SEÑORAS Piso 1º

c A. ADAME TORRES PESCADERIA TLF. PTO. 106

9 What services are
offered here?

a
SE COLOCAN CREMALLERAS

b SE REVELAN FOTOS DE COLOR

c
SE HACEN LLAVES EN UN MINUTO

10 What do these signs tell you
about opening hours?

a TANCAT

b SABADO TARDE NO CERRAMOS

c HORARIO CONTINUADO DE 10 MAÑANA A 8 TARDE ABIERTO MEDIODIA

Can that be right?

11 Eating out and drinking

Key words

casa
(house, home)

casera homely, home-made

cocina
(cooking, kitchen)

comer
(to eat)

comedor dining room
comida meal, food
comidas caseras home-cooking
comida para llevar take-away food

hielo
(ice, i.e. for cooling)

helado ice cream
heladería ice cream parlour

plato
(dish)

plato combinado set dish
plato preparado ready-prepared dish

Important words

aquí (here) and **hay** (there is, there are)
tell you that something is available

If you want a meal

The two main meals of the day are
served fairly late depending on region –
almuerzo or **comida** (it means 'lunch' as
well as 'meal') from about 1 pm until
4 pm, and **cena** (supper) from about
8 pm onwards.

The rating of eating places is often
shown by the number of 'forks', e.g. four
forks tell you it's a very good restaurant
but not cheap!

Restaurante is an obvious place for a
meal.
Bar-restaurante provides bar service as
well as meals.
Hostería is an inn or hostelry which
provides food and sometimes
accommodation.

For a family-type eating place look for
mesón, posada or **fonda**, all meaning
'inn', though this isn't indicative of their
price range.

conde count

If it says **venta** it's a roadside inn though elsewhere **venta** means 'sale'. Some eating places are called **casa**, e.g. **Casa Pepe**. Others just display their name and list their specialities (**especialidades**).

Places advertising **comidas** or **comidas caseras** usually offer inexpensive meals. So do many bars, café-bars and **chiringuitos** (temporary open-air restaurants) which you find on many beaches.

Menus

If you want to study the menu look for **carta**.

Most eating places provide a **menú** (fixed price meal), sometimes headed **menú del día** or **menú de la casa**. As a rule this includes bread (**pan**), wine (**vino**) and dessert (**postre**).

Very popular and inexpensive are **platos combinados**. These are set dishes which can combine anything from a fried egg (**huevo frito**), chicken (**pollo**), potatoes (**patatas**) to fish (**pescado**) and salad (**ensalada**) – all on one plate.

If you want to find out what the day's special is look for **especial de hoy** (**hoy** = today).

A sign with **local climatizado** informs you that the premises are air-conditioned.

Self-service

Look for **cafetería, autoservicio** (self-service *not* a car service) and **buffet libre** (one where you can have second helpings).

Take-away meals and picnics

If you want to buy ready-prepared dishes look for **platos preparados**. The food departments of some big stores sell hot and cold dishes and so do some delicatessen shops.

Take-away meals are advertised as **comidas para llevar** (**llevar** = to take away) or **para la calle** (literally 'for the street'). A popular take-away food is **pollo asado** (roast chicken).

Sometimes you can have a drink and bring your own food where it says **se admiten comidas**.

If you're picnicking and want to keep your food cool, look for signs advertising **hielo** (ice), particularly at service stations.

Occasionally when you've found the ideal spot for a picnic you may be unlucky and see this sign:

este recinto this site

cubitos small cubes
saquito small bag
Sahy name of firm

Snacks

For typical Spanish snack food look for a **marisquería** which sells prawns (**gambas**) and other cooked shellfish (**mariscos**), or a **freiduría** which sells fried fish.

The snacks universally eaten with drinks are **tapas**. They can be anything from **gambas** to titbits of fish, sausage (**salchicha**), ham (**jamón**), Spanish omelette (**tortilla**) served on small plates. Bigger portions are described as **raciones**.

chacina pork meats
serrana from the mountains

Many small places and stalls sell **perros calientes** or **perritos calientes** (hot dogs), **bocadillos** (filled rolls or sandwiches), **hamburguesas** (hamburgers), **burguer** (burgers), **patatas fritas** (crisps or chips), **palomitas** (salted popcorn).

Light refreshments

If you fancy an ice cream look for signs with **helados** or **heladería**. There's usually a wide choice of flavours, e.g. **vainilla** (vanilla), **fresa** (strawberry), **nata** (cream). A speciality worth trying is **tarta helada** (ice cream cake).

Favourite mid-morning or afternoon pastries are **churros** – long pieces of dough fried in oil, with or without icing sugar on top. They're sold at stalls, in cafés and **churrerías** and are best when freshly made.

For cakes (**tartas**) and pastries (**pasteles**) with coffee (**café**) or tea (**té**) go to a **pastelería**, **café** or **café-bar**. Many also serve **meriendas**, light meals taken in the late afternoon, often consisting of **bocadillos**.

If you want breakfast

Look for signs with **desayuno** (breakfast). The most likely place serving it is either a café or a bar. A Spanish-style breakfast consists of **café** with or without milk (**leche**), **tostadas** (toast), **suizos** (buns) or pastries which are regional specialities and often **churros**.

prueba proof
buen gusto good taste

Drinks

Look for signs with **bebidas** (drinks) or **refrescos** (cold drinks). Coke is **cola**, *n o t* to be confused with **cola (de) toro** meaning oxtail, or more precisely bull's tail.

Ondina
name of a soft drink

Drinks with crushed ice are **granizados**, orange juice is **zumo de naranja**.
A popular summer drink is **horchata**, made from **chufa** nuts.
Milk shakes are **batidos**, and a good place to get them is a **lechería** (milk bar).
A **chocolatería** serves **chocolate** (chocolate drinks *n o t* chocolates).

fría cold

If you want a place specialising in beer (**cerveza**) look for a **cervecería**. **Cerveza a presión** or **cerveza de(l) barril** means they sell draught beer. A **caña** is a small glass of beer, a **tanque** a large one.

The obvious place for wine and spirits as well as beer is a **bar**, a **taberna** or the more old-fashioned **tasca**.

To enjoy local wines (**vinos del país**) look for a **bodega**. This one specialises in sherry which comes from the Jerez region.

Apart from snack food (**tapas y raciones** see p. 81) many bars serve light meals, coffee and soft drinks.

Opening hours

There are no licensing hours, so eating places and bars can stay open very late. Bars usually open early in the morning. Many close on Sundays if there are not many customers around.
Eating places may close one day a week to give their staff (**personal**) a rest (**descanso**).

❷ Test yourself

1 Identify these 'false friends': **local   raciones**

2 How many places that sell food or drinks ending in ... **(e)ría** can you list?

3 What would you expect to find if you followed these signs?

a   b   c

4 You'd like a snack. What do these places offer?

a PASTELERIA HELADOS HORCHATA

b TARTA HELADA "Especialidad de la Casa"

c LaCabaña COCINA RAPIDA Y PASTELERIA

d BOCADILLOS CALIENTES

e HAY CHOCOLATE VIRGEN DE LOS REYES Y CHURROS MAÑANA Y TARDE

f PERRITOS CALIENTES 50 HAMBURGUESAS 80

5 What does it say here about food?

a SE ADMITEN COMIDAS

b RESTAURANTE COMIDAS PARA LLEVAR

c CAFE-BAR Los GERANIOS ESPECIALIDADES COMIDAS CASERAS PLATOS COMBINADOS TAPAS VARIADAS Y RACIONES

6 It's a hot day. You'd like a drink. What are the choices?

a POLLOS VINOS del PAIS RIVEIRO-RIOJAS CERVEZAS COLAS Y REFRESCOS

b HAY CERVEZA Y REFRESCO VINOS

e GRANIZADOS LIMON HORCHATA

c HAY COLA TORO

d CHOCOLATERIA LECHERIA del postigo

7 You want to try a Spanish omelette. Which looks the best bet?

a AQUI: TAPAS VARIADAS PULPO, EMPANADA, TORTILLA, ENSALADA. E.T.C

b CAFE-BAR-RESTAURANTE LA LANZADA HABITACIONES – MARISCOS Y COCINA REGIONAL

c VINOS TAPAS Y COMIDAS

8 You want to have breakfast.
  Will any of these places do?

a

b

c

9 What do these signs say?

a

b

c

10 What does it say here about
   opening and closing times?

a

b

11 You often see this sign on the door
   of eating and other places.
   What does it mean?

Can that be right?

12 Looking for a loo

🔑 Key word

servicios   **serveis** (in Catalonia)
(loos)

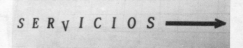

Names for loos

The usual descriptions are **WC** (but see below), **servicio(s)** or **aseos**. Other names you may come across are **lavabos** and **retrete**. **Urinario** is a urinal.

Women look for **señoras** or **S**, occasionally **WS** which is short for **water señoras** – **water** being the popular name for a loo.
Men look for **caballeros** or **C**, or sometimes **WC** (**water caballeros**) – but only when there's also a **WS**! Elsewhere **WC** simply indicates public lavatories.

As public lavatories are few and far between, nobody seems to mind if you make use of **servicios** in a bar!
Be wary of **servicio** or **servicios** on signs at garages and service stations. It usually tells you that they provide servicing.

What it costs

Most loos are free of charge (**gratuito**). Slot machines to operate loo doors are rare. If there's an attendant (**empleado**) it's usual to leave a small tip. There may be notices saying you should ask (**pida** or **pidan**) for paper (**papel**) or soap (**jabón**).

POR FAVOR
PIDAN PAPEL
AL EMPLEADO.
Gracias

❓ Test yourself

1 You're looking for the loo. Which are 'gents' and which are 'ladies'?

a
SEÑORAS

b CABALLEROS

c `SERVICIOS C.`

d `SERVICIOS S`

2 Which of these signs points
   the way to a loo?

a SERVICIOS DE SEÑORAS y CABALLEROS

b ESTACION DE SERVICIO Nº 7128

c (T) TALBOT — SERVICIO 400 Mts.

d SERVICIOS

e LAVABOS

f ASEOS

3 What's the difference between
   these two signs?

a SERVICIOS TELEFONICOS

b SERVICIOS Y TELEFONOS

4 These loos have shower facilities
   (**servicio de duchas**). What are you
   asked to do?

W.C
POR FAVOR.
PARA EL SERVICIO
DE DUCHAS.
PIDAN JABON AL
EMPLEADO.
        Gracias
SERVICIO GRATUITO

Can that be right?

Oh dear! Loos closed on Sundays and public holidays!

DOMINGO Y FESTIVO SIN SERVICIO

13 If you feel ill (see also chapter 14)

🔵 Key words

ambulatorio
(state health centre)

consulta
(surgery)

horas de consulta surgery hours
consultorio consulting room, surgery

farmacia
(dispensing chemist's)

farmacia de guardia, farmacia de servicio
chemist's on duty
servicio farmacéutico dispensing service

sanitario
(medical, health ...)

auxilio sanitario medical aid
A.T.S. = ayudante técnico sanitario nurse
practitioner; small surgery run by **A.T.S.**
sector sanitario medical room

socorro
(help, aid)

casa (de) socorro first aid station, casualty
department
puesto (de) socorro first aid post

urgencia
(emergency)

servicio de urgencia emergency service or
treatment
urgencias emergency treatment

If you need medicine or a simple remedy

Look for **farmacia** or for the red or green
cross you can often spot from afar. Every
farmacia sells proprietary drugs,
medicines (**medicamentos**), ointments,
bandages, etc., and dispenses doctor's
prescriptions (**recetas**). Some also sell a
limited range of toiletries and cosmetics.

When the chemist's is closed, a notice
with **servicio farmacéutico**, **farmacia de
guardia** or **farmacia de servicio** tells you
which one is on duty and when.

Don't be misled by **droguería** – they
don't sell drugs, but household goods,
toiletries, etc.

turnos on duty

If you need medical attention

For medical attention or prescriptions you can go to an **ambulatorio**. Treatment is free for EC citizens. You must have your DSS form E111 with you and register first with the **Seguridad Social** (state health service).

Close to markets and shops you'll often see signs with **A.T.S. (ayudante(s) técnico(s) sanitario(s))** or **practicante** (practitioner). They mark small surgeries run by qualified nursing staff (usually just one man) where you can have routine treatment such as injections, bandaging, blood pressure checks. They are mostly open during shopping hours. Fees are modest.

On campsites a door marked **botiquín** means there is a first aid kit or room. **Primeros auxilios** means first aid is given.

In public places such as railway stations you can get help where it says **sector sanitario**. Elsewhere look for **puesto (de) socorro** (first aid post).

If you need to find a hospital

Follow the white on blue **H** (not the **H** symbol for hotel, see p. 48) or signs with **hospital**, **casa de socorro** (casualty department, first aid station) or **clínica** (private hospital). Emergency treatment (**servicio de urgencia**) is usually free, but unlikely to be so in a **clínica** unless there is a sign **Seguridad Social**.

If you're looking for a doctor

On a nameplate **Doctor** or **Dr. (Doctora** or **Dra.** if it's a woman) doesn't always indicate a doctor of medicine — it could for example be a lawyer (**abogado**). If it says **médico** it's sure to be a doctor.

cirugía surgery, i.e. surgical treatment

89

Many advertise the fact that they are specialists, e.g. **médico cirujano** (surgeon), **médico de niños** (paediatrician) or tell you which areas of disease (**enfermedad**) they specialise in.

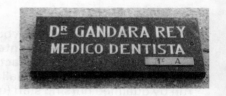

If you have toothache

You need to find a **dentista**, a **médico dentista** or a **clínica dental** (dental practice, not a clinic).

Urgencias means they will give you emergency treatment.

Surgery hours

These are rarely given on nameplates. Where they are given it will say **días** or **horas de consulta**. Any mention of **cita** or **petición** means you have to make an appointment. Most doctors and specialists have surgeries in the late afternoon or early evening.

❷ Test yourself

1 Identify these 'false friends':
consulta droguería sanitario

2 You've been given the address of a skin specialist. Which one is it?

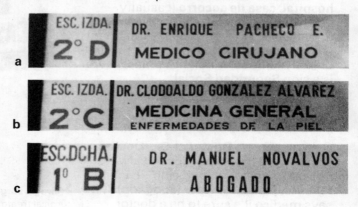

ESC. IZDA.
2° D
a

DR. ENRIQUE   PACHECO   E.
MEDICO   CIRUJANO

ESC. IZDA.
2° C
b

DR. CLODOALDO GONZALEZ ALVAREZ
MEDICINA GENERAL
ENFERMEDADES DE LA PIEL

ESC.DCHA.
1° B
c

DR. MANUEL   NOVALVOS
ABOGADO

3 You've got a nasty graze. Can any of these places help?

a

b

c

d

e

4 What is the essence of this notice (**aviso**)?

AVISO

La Farmacia de Servicio de Urgencia, a partir de las 10 de la noche, SOLAMENTE dispensará medicamentos con receta médica

5 You want 'casualty'. Which sign would you follow?

a

b

Hospital
VIRGEN DEL VALLE

c

Ambulatorio

d

Can that be right?

Another casualty department?!

14 Dangers and emergencies
(see also chapter 13)

🙂 Key words

no tocar don't touch

incendio
(fire)

peligro   **peligro de muerte** mortal danger
(danger)   **peligroso** dangerous

socorro   **casa (de) socorro** first aid station,
                    casualty department
                    puesto (de) socorro first aid post
                    salida de socorro emergency exit

urgencia
(emergency)

Steering clear of danger

Signs with **peligro** and **peligroso** warn
you of serious danger. Don't bathe for
instance where it says **peligroso bañarse**
(bathing dangerous) (see p. 67). Don't
touch where you see **no tocar**.

You are alerted to lesser dangers by
signs with **atención**, **cuidado**, **precaución**
all meaning 'caution', 'beware'.

maquinaria pesada heavy machinery

If things go wrong

You may need to find the emergency
exit. Look for **salida de emergencia**,
salida de urgencia or, particularly in
buses, **salida de socorro**.

You may need police help. Watch out for
signs with **guardia civil** in rural areas and
small communities, at frontier posts,
railway stations, harbours, and along
roads and motorways.

In towns look for **policía**, **policía
nacional**, **policía municipal**, **policía de
tráfico** or **comisaría** (police station).

Fire hazards

There is a serious risk of forest fires in Spain, particularly during the long hot summer. Signs like this warn you to take care. Some even remind you not to throw cigarette ends (**colillas**) out of the car. Signs with **uso bomberos** (**bomberos** = fire brigade) indicate points to which fire hoses can be connected.

Don't be misled by this sign: there's no danger of fire – it means you mustn't park because you will obstruct access to a fire hydrant.

In case of accident

Make for **casa (de) socorro** (first aid station or casualty department) unless you happen to spot a first aid post (**puesto (de) socorro** or **puesto de primeros auxilios**). Most are run by the Spanish Red Cross (**Cruz Roja Española**) who can also provide an ambulance (see also p. 89).

primeros auxilios first aid
evacuación transport to hospital, etc

Calling the emergency services

For the **policía** and **guardia civil** dial 091, for the **policía municipal** 092.
In case of fire call the **servicio de bomberos**. For urgent medical attention ring the **Casa de Socorro**, the **Servicio de Urgencia de la Seguridad Social** or the **Cruz Roja**. Phone numbers for these vary from place to place. You can ask **Información** on 003 free of charge for the number of the service you want. To call the emergency services from a phone box you need a minimum of ten pesetas (see p. 55).

There are phones for use in emergencies on many major roads and all motorways (see pp. 25, 34).

❓ Test yourself

1 You need first aid.
  Where can you get help?

2 What's the message on these signs?

3 No parking. Why?

4 This sign is incomplete.
  Try and work out its meaning.

Can that be right?

Answers to 'Test yourself' questions

Making sense of signs

1 and 2 (Words in brackets give you the clue to the signs.)

(i) **e** 'respect, i.e. keep off, the garden' (**respeten**);   (ii) **a** 'entrance through No. 14, thank you' (**gracias**) and **d** 'please use the waste bins' (**por favor**);   (iii) **c** 'don't smoke at the counter (**no**);   (iv) **f** 'parking prohibited – private property' (**prohibido**);   (v) **b** 'not working', i.e. out of order (**no**);   (vi) **g** 'beware of the dogs' (**cuidado**).

3 and 4

(i) **c** 'entrance only, exit through checkout – no dogs';   (ii) **e** 'open Saturday afternoons'; (iii) **b** 'car park – post office';   (iv) **d** 'rooms available';   (v) **a** 'exhibition rooms – first floor'.

5   **a** for your convenience please leave (**deposite**) your shopping bags and parcels in the cloakroom;   **b** don't sit down (**prohibido sentarse**) – private property;   **c** serve yourself (**sírvase**) and pay (**pague**) at the cash desk;   **d** don't throw (**no tirar**) cigarette ends on the floor;   **e** no entry (**prohibido el paso**) – private estate.

7   please note: new opening hours from Monday 30th September – Monday to Saturday, mornings 9.30–1.30, afternoons 5–8.

---

1   1 former; office; manager's office; private; floor; press.   **2** (i) town – caution;   (ii) way through or across – avenue;   (iii) door – harbour.   **3 a** path, way;   **b** short street linking two others;   **c** passage, alley.   **4** no, it takes you to the even numbers.   **5** exit this way, you're on level 1.   **6 a** third;   **b** ground floor.   **7** to the first floor, then to the right.   **8 b** (**a** means it's private and you can't go in).   **9 a** entrance to the Alhambra (Moorish palace in Granada);   **b** Prado avenue (**po.** = **paseo**), buses;   **c** post office;   **d** church;   **e** railway station;   **f** access for pedestrians to car park (**alameda vieja** = old park).   **10 a** press (button) for the floor you want (**deseada** = desired);   **b** not to enter; **c** push;   **d** enter without knocking.   **11 e** (**a** is a pedestrian precinct,   **b** a bullring, **c** a cul-de-sac,   **d** a block).   *Can that be right?* Wet paint! (**pinta** = someone is painting)

2a   1 coach; trolley; traffic; to drive; car; chauffeur; private.   **2** (i) seat belt – ring road; (ii) shortened forms for **puerta** city gate, **puente** bridge, **puerto** harbour, port. **3 a** harbour, car parks;   **b** town centre via Generalísimo bridge;   **c** nurserymen; **d** centre of a small town;   **e** campsite, beach (**playa**), N–IV trunk road.   **4 a** (**b** is a cul-de-sac,   **c** a bypass, Cobisa is a place name).   **5 a** keep out of bus lane (**dejen libre** = leave free);   **b** please drive carefully;   **c** don't block the junction;   **d** observe 30 km/h speed limit on entire housing estate.   **6 a** pedestrians crossing;   **b** sunken verges; **c** falling stones;   **d** lorries emerging;   **e** bad road surface for 10 kms;   **f** brow of a hill. **7 a** no entry;   **b** no coaches or lorries except for loading (**carga**) and unloading (**descarga**).   **8 a** road closed 100 metres ahead, diversion;   **b** road C-404 leading to Navalcarnero and Ciempozuelos, change of direction 1 kilometre ahead (i.e. swing right, then turn left);   **c** river La Rocina;   **d** lane marked with a cross is closed, lane marked with an arrow is open (dual language sign, in Catalan and Spanish).   *Can that be right?* Sign to motorail, not a road.

2b 1 coaches; cars; motorbikes; level; collect; private car.　**2 a** car park with attendant (Mi Casita – name of restaurant);　**b** 'pay and display' parking meter;　**c** 'blue zone', maximum stay one hour.　**3 a** yes, side by side;　**b** no, for coaches and hire cars;　**c** no, for motorbikes;　**d** yes.　**4 a** residents;　**b** authorised cars;　**c** railway station users for one hour.　**5 a** any day except market days;　**b** between 2 pm and 7 am;　**c** and **d** from the 1st to the 15th of the month.　**6 a** full, drive on (**siga** = continue);　**b** take your ticket;　**c** for season ticket holders;　**d** exit on level 3.　**7 a** no parking on both sides of the road;　**b** if you park, your car may be towed away (**aviso** = warning);　**c** parking for private cars limited to 1½ hours on weekdays between 9 am and 8 pm, restricted parking zone, parking disc must be displayed;　**d** private entrance to hotel, no parking;　**e** no parking in this avenue.　*Can that be right?* Parking is on the lower level.

2c **1 a** Barcelona and Girona via the A-17 motorway;　**b** exit 2 to Utrera, N–IV trunk road and Los Palacios 500 metres ahead;　**c** last service area, open 24 hours;　**d** you're on the A-49, 50 kilometres from Seville;　**e** exit 8 to airport and Caça de la Selva 12 kilometres ahead;　**f** exit 4 to Jerez North and N–IV trunk road 5 kilometres ahead.　**2 a** get toll fee ready;　**b** take toll ticket.　**3** customs.　**4** the left-hand one (the other is for medical help).

2d 1 engine; two-star (petrol); repairs; four-star (petrol).　**2** when the car needs **a** water or tyre pressure checking;　**b** petrol;　**c** a repair or spare parts;　**d** washing.　**3 f** (**a** is for diesel,　**b** out of order,　**c** four-star,　**d** says they are out of two-star,　**e** two-star,　**g** two-stroke mixture).　**4** this service station is closed from 10.30 pm to 6.30 am, the nearest station open is at Costa de la Calma, on the C-719 road at kilometre 18, 10.3 kilometres from here.　**5 c** and **d** (**a** does mechanical repairs only,　**b** is a driving school).　**6 a** towing, car removal;　**b** car wash, servicing, inspection and lubrication;　**c** engine tuning, tyre service, car wash, lubrication – on level 3;　**d** electrical and mechanical repairs.　*Can that be right?* It's a self-service shop called Vedra.

3 1 one-man operated (bus); connecting service, interchange; stop; platform.　**2 a** exit to the left, line 5 to the right (Canillejas and Aluche are stations at the end of the line);　**b** connecting service line 4 to Esperanza and Argüelles;　**c** entrance and ticket offices.　**3 b** yes, if you have the right change (**a** is for passengers with a ticket).　**4 a** is the entrance (**b** boarding prohibited).　**5 a** horsedrawn cabs;　**b** small single-decker bus;　**c** taxis (limited to two – at the airport);　**d** bus, night service (**E.M.T.** = **Empresa Municipal de Transportes**, Municipal Transport Board.)　*Can that be right?* Sevilla is a station on the Madrid underground.

4 1 modest station buffet/bar; carriage; ticket office; long; bookstall; sale; platform.　**2 b** (**a** is for local travel).　**3 a** sleeper, i.e. beds;　**b** buffet car;　**c** couchettes.　**4** arrival times of long-distance trains, type of train, coming from, platform.　**5 a** motorail;　**b** way to the platforms;　**c** exit, platform 5.　**6** (i) **c**;　(ii) **a**;　(iii) **e**;　(iv) **b**;　(v) **d**.　**7** yes, it says **estación Renfe** (railway station) (Génova – name of street).　*Can that be right?* **F.C.** is short for **ferrocarril** (railway).

5 1 room; modest hotel; boarding house.　**2** campsite – field, countryside.　**3 a** boarding house;　**b** flatlets with service;　**c** modest hotel without restaurant;　**d** hotel without restaurant;　**e** guest house;　**f** inn.　**4 a** rooms on the third floor;　**b** rooms and flats.　**5 a** rooms with bath;　**b** swimming pool, garden, dining room;　**c** bar, food and lodging;　**d** rooms and meals;　**e** furnished flat.　**6 a** laundry room and sinks for washing up;　**b** a place to wash clothes only;　**c** hot showers;　**d** drinking water;

e a place to wash crockery only; **f** men's showers.   **7 a** no cars allowed in after midnight;   **b** please note: no entry for non-campers, ask at reception (**infórmese** = ask for information) – silence, no car traffic between 12.30 am and 7.30 am;   **c** no entry for persons not camping here.   *Can that be right?* It's a sign to the campsite only (**sólo** = only).

6   **1** phone booth; letters; registered mail; phone call.   **2 a** and **c** (**b** is for stamp collectors).   **3** the slot on the right (**extranjero** = abroad).   **4 a** (**b** is for collecting parcels,   **c** for registered inland mail).   **5 a** post office savings bank;   **b** barber's shop and bar.   **6** use 25 peseta coins for intercity and national calls.   **7** on weekdays from 9 am to 1 pm and 5 pm to 9 pm (closed Sundays and public holidays).   *Can that be right?* It's a box for mail to these premises only.

7   **1 a**; **b**; **d** (**c** is a building society).   **2 a** from September 16th to June 19th open Mondays–Thursdays from 8.30 am–4.30 pm, Fridays from 8.30 am–2 pm, Saturdays 8.30 am–1 pm;   **b** open on weekdays from 9 am to 1.30 pm, on Saturdays and the day before a public holiday from 9 am to 1 pm;   **c** on the 31st the bank will open from 9 am to 12 noon.   **3** no (**no devuelve cambio** = no change given) (the instructions read: 'Insert coins for required parking time'.)   *Can that be right?* It used to be a drive-in bank.

8   **1** exhibition; royal.   **2** (i) Castile – castle;   (ii) room, hall – way out.   **3 a** parish church and walled part of the town;   **b** hermitage of Our Lady of Lanzada (place name), Romanesque art;   **c** old cathedral, Santa María quarter;   **d** castle, tourist office;   **e** Roman city called Itálica.   **4 a** parish church of Santa Catalina and town hall;   **b** 15th century castle of Santiago;   **c** opening times of the Castle of the Christian Monarchs.   **5 a** museum of fine arts;   **b** chapel of Montserrat.   **6 a** entrance to the royal palaces;   **b** way up the tower;   **c** exit at the back.   **7 a** not to take photographs;   **b** not to smoke – and be quiet (**guarde** = keep);   **c** not to sit down;   **d** not to walk on the grass.
8 a welcome to the town of Sanlúcar de Barrameda;   **b** the town of Moguer invites you to visit the Convent of Santa Clara, the Convent of San Francisco, the house and museum of Juan Ramón and Zenobia (i.e. of the Spanish poet Juan Ramón Jiménez and his wife Zenobia);   **c** you're on the wine route and entering the town of Puerto de Santa María.

9   **1** daily; boat; seats; beach.   **2** swimming pool.   **3** (i) men's showers, cubicles, cloakroom (for leaving clothes – it's **guardarropa**, not **guardarropia**, misspelt on sign); (ii) **a** you should shower before entering the swimming pool;   **b** you should not go this way wearing shoes.   **4** bars, sun shelters, loos, showers, changing rooms (Valdelagrana – name of beach).   **5 a** ten-pin (American-style) bowling;   **b** sports area;   **c** tennis, clay pigeon shooting, swimming.   **6** get tokens at the ticket office.   **7 a** (the management) reserves the right to refuse admission (**derecho** = right);   **b** for members only.   **8 b** (**a** is for even numbers).   **9** you can see flamenco dancing every day but Sunday (**Exmo. Ayuntamiento Córdoba** = the most excellent town council of Córdoba).   **10 a** you can buy bullfight tickets for the sunny or shady side of the ring;   **b** you can buy tickets for the football match.   *Can that be right?* It's called the beach of Our Lady.

10   **1** self-service (shop); cigarettes; convenience; ready-made clothes; shop selling household goods, toiletries etc; bookshop, bookstall; floor, level; souvenirs; repairs.   **2 a** and **b** (**c** is a butcher's shop which also sells cooked meats and cheeses (Consolación – name of shop, **abierto todo el año** = open all year).   **3 a** eggs and chickens;   **b** meat, cooked meats and cheeses, frozen foods, fruit and vegetables, bread, cakes, general foodstuffs – all on the ground floor.   **4 a** discount (**bolsos playa** = beach bags);   **b** reductions and attractive prices (**por falta de tallas y colores** = odd sizes and colours);   **c** special offer (**normal** = ordinary).   **5 a** market selling handicrafts, entry free of charge (**zoco** = market place);   **b** souvenirs of Madrid;   **c** gifts (also sells books, stationery and newspapers). **6 a** ladies' shoes;   **b** men's suits.   **7 a** serve yourself;   **b** cleaning materials; **c** express checkout, maximum 10 items;   **d** no admission with bags or large parcels. **8 b** (**a** is a dry cleaner's, **c** a fishmonger's).   **9 a** zips fitted;   **b** colour films developed; **c** keys cut on the spot.   **10 a** closed;   **b** open Saturday afternoons (**no cerramos** = we don't close);   **c** open all day from 10 am to 8 pm, open midday (i.e. lunchtime).   *Can that be right?* **Catsup** means 'ketchup' (**mostaza** = mustard, **vinos comunes** = table wines).

11 **1** premises; portions.   **2** eleven: **cafetería, cervecería, chocolatería, churrería, freiduría, hamburguesería, heladería, hostería, lechería, marisquería, pastelería.** There is also **horchatería** (see question 8).   **3 a** entrance to self-service restaurant;   **b** dining room; **c** temporary beach restaurant and bar.   **4 a** cakes, pastries, ice creams, **horchata;   b** ice cream cake, speciality of the house;   **c** fast food, cakes and pastries;   **d** toasted sandwiches;   **e** chocolate drinks and **churros**, mornings and afternoons;   **f** hot dogs, hamburgers.   **5 a** you can bring your own food;   **b** take-away meals;   **c** home-cooking, set dishes, choice of small and large bar snacks.   **6 a** local wines, beer, coke and cold drinks;   **b** wine, beer and cold drinks;   **d** chocolate and milk drinks;   **e** crushed ice drinks, lemon drinks, **horchata**   (**c** not a drink, but an advert for oxtail).   **7 a** offers **tortilla** (**pulpo** = octopus, **empanada** = pie) (**b** offers rooms, shellfish and regional cooking,   **c** wines, snacks and meals).   **8** yes, **a** and **b** both offer **desayunos** (**quesos manchegos** = cheeses from La Mancha) (**c** offers **horchata**).   **9 a** sells hamburgers and roast chickens;   **b** roadside inn called 'The Chicken';   **c** ice sold here.   **10 a** closed to give the staff time off;   **b** closed in the afternoons from 5 to 7.   **11** air-conditioned premises.   *Can that be right?* **Raciones** are large portions of bar snacks.

12 **1 a** and **d** are 'ladies';   **b** and **c** 'gents'.   **2 a, d, e, f** (**b** is a service station,   **c** a service garage).   **3 a** points the way to telephone services, i.e. a **telefónica;   b** to loos and telephones.   **4** ask the attendant for soap, no charge.   *Can that be right?* **Sin servicio** means there's no service at this counter.

13 **1** surgery; shop selling toiletries, household goods etc.; medical.   **2 b** (**enfermedades de la piel** = skin diseases) (**a** is a surgeon,   **c** is a lawyer).   **3 b, c, d** (**Atecsa**, same as **A.T.S.**),   **e** (**a** is a shop selling hardware, household goods, toiletries etc.).   **4** after 10 pm the chemist on emergency duty will only dispense medicines against a doctor's prescription.   **5 a** (**b** is the sign for a hotel,   **c** for an ordinary hospital,   **d** for a state health centre).   *Can that be right?* It's a maternity home.

14 **1 a** at the Spanish Red Cross first aid post 2 kilometres from here;   **b** at the Spanish Red Cross first aid post at the coach station.   **2 a** beware obstacles in the roadway, maximum speed 10 km/h;   **b** don't throw cigarette ends out of the car because of the danger of fire.   **3 a** danger, automatic door;   **b** emergency exit.   **4** danger, high tension wire (**alta** = high, **tensión** is missing).   *Can that be right?* **Bomberos** are the fire brigade.

Word List

The meanings listed here apply to words used on the signs included in this book. Other meanings are not listed. The numbers in brackets refer you to the page on which the word is explained more fully. Words where the meaning is obvious are omitted.

¡¡Atención!! In Spanish alphabetical order, **ch** counts as a separate letter and comes after **c**; **ll** comes after **l**, **ñ** after **n**.

a at; for; from here, ahead; to; until, with
A = autopista; parador
a partir de (as) from
abierto, -a open
abogado lawyer
abonados season ticket holders
abril April
abrimos we open
ac., acc. = accessorio additional; business premises
acceso access, entrance
aceite oil
admisión acceptance; admission
aduana customs
aeropuerto airport
agencia de viajes travel agency
agente único one-man operated
agua water
ahorros savings
aire air
ajeno, -a not belonging
al at the; (from) the; of the; on to the; to (the); for the
al paso at walking pace, slowly
alcázar (Moorish) castle, palace
alimentación (alimen.) food department, food shop
alimento food
almuerzo lunch
alquíla(n)se 'to let'
alquiler hire
alta high

ambos both
ambulatorio state health centre
amodiño carefully (Galician)
amueblado furnished
amurallado walled
andén platform
antes de before
anticipada in advance
antiguo, -a former
año year
aparcadero car park
aparcamiento car park; parking space
aparcar (to) park
aquí here; served here
área area, zone; service area
arroyo small river
artesanía handicrafts
artículos (art.) items, articles
asado roast
ascensor lift
aseos cloakrooms, loos
AT = apartamentos
ATECSA = A.T.S.
atención beware! mind! caution! please note
atracciones amusements
A.T.S. = ayudante(s) técnico(s) sanitario(s) nurse practitioner(s); small surgery (89)
auto car
auto expreso motorail (44)
autobanco drive-in bank (58)
autobús bus
autocar coach
automóvil motor car
automovilista motorist

autopista (A) motorway
autoservicio self-service (shop or restaurant)
auxilio(s) help, aid
auxilio sanitario medical aid
avería breakdown
aviso warning
ayudante técnico sanitario (A.T.S.) nurse practitioner (89)
ayuntamiento town council, town hall
azul blue

bajada way down
bajo, -a low
balneario bathing establishment
banca, banco bank
banco hipotecario building society
bañarse to bathe
baño bath; bathing
barbería barber's
bares bars
barrio (old) quarter; district
basura rubbish
bellas artes fine arts
bicis = bicicletas bicycles
bienvenido welcome
billete ticket; bank note
blanco, -a white
bloquear (to) block
bocadillos sandwiches, filled rolls
bodega place selling local wines, wine bar
bolera bowling (alley)
bolsa, bolso (shopping) bag
bomberos fire brigade

botiquín first aid room; first aid kit
buen good
buzón letterbox

C = caballeros; carretera comarcal
caballero man, (for) men
caballeros men; men's; 'gents'
caballo horse
cabina phone booth; cubicle
café café; coffee
cafetería buffet car; cafeteria
caja cash desk; cashier's; checkout; type of bank; banking hours
caja postal post office savings bank
cajero automático cash dispenser
caliente hot; toasted
calzado wearing shoes
calzados footwear, shoes
calle (c., c/) street, road
calle cebra street where pedestrians have priority
calle peatonal pedestrian precinct
calle sin salida cul-de-sac
callejón narrow street
camas beds; sleeper
cambio change; exchange; exchange rate
cambio de rasante brow of a hill
cambio de sentido change of direction, turning off (24)
camino path, way
camiones lorries
campamento campsite
camping campsite
campistas campers
campo countryside; field, ground
cantina small station buffet (46)
capilla chapel
carga loading
carne(s) meat
carnicería butcher's shop

carretera (ctra.) road; main road; roadway
carretera comarcal (C) main road
carretera nacional (CN, N) trunk road
carril lane
carrito, carro (shopping) trolley
cartas letters
casa house; home; museum
casa de huéspedes guest house
case (de) socorro casualty department, first aid station
casera home-made
Castilla Castile
castillo castle
catsup ketchup
cena supper
centro (in the) centre; (town) centre
centro comercial shopping centre
cercanías local and suburban travel
cerrado, -a closed
cerramos we close
certificados registered mail
cervecería bar specialising in beer
cerveza beer
césped grass, lawn
CH = casa de huéspedes
cierren close!
cigarrillos cigarettes; cigarette ends
cinturón de seguridad seat belt
circulación traffic
circular to drive
circule(n) drive!
circunvalación bypass
cirujano surgeon
cita appointment
ciudad town, city
climatizado air-conditioned
clínica private hospital, clinic; practice
CN = carretera nacional
cocina cooking; kitchen
cocina rápida fast food

coche car; vehicle; carriage
coche camas sleeper
coche de caballo horsedrawn cab
cola 'coke'
cola (de) toro bull's tail (i.e. oxtail)
colillas cigarette ends
comedor dining room
comer to eat
comestibles groceries, provisions
comida meal, food, lunch
comida para llevar take-away food
comidas caseras home cooking
comodidad convenience
completo full
compra purchase; 'we buy'
comunes ordinary
con with
concurso competition
conductor driver, chauffeur
confecciones ready-to-wear clothing
conferencia phone call
confitería confectionery; sweetshop, confectioner's
congelados frozen foods
congreso congress, meeting
consigna cloakroom (for leaving things)
consulta surgery (hours)
continuado continuous
correo mail
correos post office
correspondencia connection, interchange
corrida = corrida de toros bullfight
cortado, -a closed, blocked
corto short
cremalleras zips
cristianos Christian
cruce junction; cross!
cruz cross
cuidado beware! careful! mind!

charcutería (shop selling) cooked meats and cheeses

cheques travellers cheques
chiringuito temporary (open-air) restaurant
chocolate chocolate drinks
chocolatería shop selling chocolate drinks
chufa tiger nut
churrería shop selling churros
churros pieces of dough fried in oil (82)

dcha. = derecha right (hand side)
de of; for; from; about; by
de la of the; in the
de las, de los of the
dejen leave!
del of the; from (the)
delantera front
delegación local branch
deporte(s) sport(s)
deportivo, -a sports..., for sports
deposite leave! insert!
derecho right
desayuno breakfast
descanso rest
descarga unloading
descuento reduction, discount
deseado, -a desired
despacio slowly
despacho issue (of tickets); office; ticket office
desprendimiento coming loose (i.e. falling stones)
destino destination
desvío diversion
devuelve returns
día day
diario daily
días azules 'blue days' (45)
dinero money
dirección manager's office, management; direction
disco parking disc
discos records
dispensará will dispense
divisas (foreign) currency
domingo (on) Sunday(s)
dos two

droguería (shop selling) household goods, toiletries etc.
ducha shower
dúchese take a shower

el the
electricidad electrical repairs
embarcación boat
empleado attendant
empresa enterprise
empujad push!
en at; at the; for; in; on, wearing
en batería side by side
en servicio open
engrase lubrication
ensalada salad
entrada entrance, entry; entrance fee, admission ticket; admission; way in
entrar to enter
entrega delivery
equipajes luggage
ermita hermitage
esc. = escalera stairs
escalón lateral verge below road level
escuela school
especialidad speciality; 'we specialise'
especialidades (our) specialities
espera waiting
esquí acuático water skiing
está (you) are; it is
estación (est.) (railway) station; stop
estacionamiento (estacio.) car park; parking
estacionar to park
estado state, condition
estanco tobacconist's (73)
este this
evitar to avoid
ex(c)mo. = excelentísimo the most excellent
expendedor (ticket) dispenser
exposición exhibition
expreso type of train (44)
extranjero abroad

F = fonda
facturación registration (for luggage etc.)
falta lack, shortage
farmacia de servicio chemist's on duty
ferretería hardware (shop)
ferrocarril (F.C.) railway
ferrocarriles (FF.CC.) railways
festivo public holiday; non-working day
festivos Sundays and public holidays
fichas tokens
fiesta party, festival, festivity; public holiday
fijo fixed
filatélico for stamp collectors
fin end
finca estate
fonda inn
fondo back
fotos films, photographs
fregadero kitchen sink
freiduría shop selling fried fish
fría cold
frito fried
frutería fruit and vegetables, greengroceries; greengrocer's
fumar (to) smoke
fume smoke!
funciona functions, works
fútbol football
fútbol sala five-a-side football

garaje garage
gasóleo diesel (36)
gasóleo auto (gasóleo A) diesel for cars
gasolina petrol
gasolina 92 two-star
gasolina 97 four-star
gasolinera petrol station
gracias thank you
gran turismo hire cars and coaches
gran(des) large, big

granizados crushed ice drinks
gratuito free of charge
grúa hoist, towing vehicle
guarda guard
guardarropa cloakroom, place to leave clothes
Guardia Civil Civil Guard

h, H = hora(s)
H = hospital; hotel
habitaciones rooms
hacer fotos to take photographs
hamburguesas hamburgers
hamburguesería hamburger bar
hasta until; to
hay there is, there are; available; we have
helada frozen
heladería ice cream parlour
helado ice cream
hielo ice (for cooling)
hora (h., H) hour, o'clock
horario opening hours (76); shopping hours; times when parking restrictions apply; timetable, times
horario de caja banking hours
horas hours, times; o'clock (14)
horchata drink made from chufa nuts
horchatería place specialising in horchata drinks
hospedaje lodging, accommodation
hostal modest hotel
hostal residencia modest hotel without restaurant
hostería inn, hostelry
hotel residencia hotel without restaurant
hoy today
HR = hotel residencia
hras., hrs., hs. = horas
HS = hostal
HsR = hostal residencia
huevo egg

iglesia church
impares odd (numbers)
importe charge, fee, amount
incendio fire
inferior lower
insuperable incomparable
interesantísimos most interesting (i.e. very attractive)
interior inside, interior, indoor
interurbano intercity
introducir to insert
introduzca insert!
izquierda (izda.) left (hand side)

jabón soap
jamón ham
jardín garden
jefe head, boss, master
jerezana from the Jerez region
jóvenes young people
juego game
jueves Thursday(s)

km., kms. = kilómetros

la the
laborables weekdays, working days
lados sides
largo long
largo recorrido long-distance travel
las the
las = las . . . horas . . . o'clock
lavadero laundry room
lavado (car) wash
le you
lechería shop selling milk drinks, milk bar
libre free of charge; free, vacant; spaces available
librería bookshop, bookstall
libros books
ligero, -a light
limón lemon (drink)
limosna alms
limpieza cleaning materials; cleanliness
línea cable

línea (L) line, number, route; bus number
línea especial special service
literas couchettes
local premises
localidad(es) seat(s), ticket(s)
locutorio public telephone office
los the; on (13)
lunes Monday(s)

llamada telephone call
llamar to knock
llaves keys
llegada(s) arrival(s)
lleno full
llevar (to) take away

m = metros metres
mal bad
manzana block (of buildings)
mañana (in the) morning(s); a.m.; tomorrow
mar sea
mariscar to gather shellfish
marisco(s) shellfish
marisquería shop selling (cooked) shellfish
martes Tuesday(s)
más more; most
maternidad maternity
máximo (max.) maximum (stay)
mecánico, -a mechanical; for mechanical repairs
medicamentos medicines
médico doctor (of medicine)
médico, -a doctor's; medical
médico dentista dentist
mediodía midday, lunchtime
menores minors, people under 18
menos less
mercado market
merienda light late afternoon meal
merluza hake
mesón inn
metálico cash
metro underground railway
mezcla two-stroke mixture

microbús small bus
miércoles Wednesday(s)
minutos (min.) minutes
mismo (your)self
molestias annoyance,
    inconvenience
momentánea brief
moneda coin, currency;
    money; small change
mostrador counter
motor engine
motos = motocicletas
    motorbikes
mts. = metros metres
muerte death

N = carretera nacional;
    norte
nacionales national,
    domestic (flights)
natural fresh
neumáticos tyres
niños children
no no; not; does not; don't;
    non-
no. = número number
no funciona out of order
no pasar no entry
nocturno night ...
noche (at) night; p.m.
normal two-star petrol;
    ordinary
norte north
Ntra. = Nuestra
nuestro, -a our
nuevo new

o or
oberto, -a open (Catalan)
obligatorio compulsory
obras road works; repairs
obtener to obtain
oferta special offer
oficina office
oficina de cambio exchange
    bureau
ojo look out! (literally 'eye')
otra other

P = pensión
p. = pesetas
pago payment

pague pay!
país country, area
panadería bread shop;
    baker's shop
pantalón trousers
papeleras waste bins
papelería stationer's
paquetes parcels
para for; in order to; to
parada stop
parador state-run hotel (49)
pares even (numbers)
parking car park
parroquia parish church
parroquial parish ...
particular private
pasaje passage, alley
pasar (to) enter, go through;
    to go in; to go across
pase enter! go! pass!
pasen cross! go!
paseo trip
paseo (po.) (tree-lined) avenue
paso entry; pace, step; right
    of way; way across, way
    through; access; way in
paso inferior subway
pastelería cakes, pastries
    etc.; cake and pastry shop
patatas fritas fried potatoes;
    chips; crisps
patio courtyard
patronato board
peaje toll
peatge toll (Catalan)
peatonal pedestrian; for
    pedestrians
peatones pedestrians
peligro danger
peligroso dangerous
peluquería hairdresser's
pensión boarding house
permanente permanent,
    round the clock
permitido allowed
perritos or **perros calientes**
    hot dogs
perro dog
personal staff
pescadería fishmonger's
pescado fish
petición request

pida(n) ask for!
piel skin
pintar to paint
piscina swimming pool
pise walk on!
piso flat; floor, storey (17)
plancha grilled on a griddle
planta floor, level (17); plant
planta baja ground floor
plato dish
plato combinado set dish
    (80)
playa (pya.) beach
plaza (pl., plza., pza.) square
plaza de toros bullring
plomo lead
plza. = plaza
po. = paseo
población small town
pollo chicken
por because of; by; for; in;
    on; via; per; through(out)
por favor please
potable drinking (water)
practicante practitioner (89)
precaución beware, caution;
    take care
precio price; fare; fee,
    money
premios prizes
prensa newspapers and
    magazines; press
previa prior
primer(o), -a first
privado, -a private
procedencia place of origin,
    (coming) from
prohibido, -a forbidden,
    prohibited
propiedad property
próximo, -a next; coming;
    near
pta. = puerta
ptas., pts. = pesetas
pte. = puente
pto. = puerto; puesto
puente (pte.) bridge
puerta (pta.) city gate; door
puerto (pto.) harbour, port
Puerto ... Port ...
puesta a punto engine tuning
puesto (pto.) post; stall

puesto (de) socorro first aid post

pulse press!

pza. = plaza

quesos cheeses

R = residencia hotel without restaurant facilities (49)

raciones large portions

rápido type of train (44)

rápido, -a quick

rasante gradient

real royal

rebajas reductions, 'sale'

recambios spare parts

receta prescription

recinto enclosed area, enclosure; site

recogida collection

recoja take! collect!

recorrido distance travelled

recreativo recreational, for recreation

recuerdos souvenirs

red network

refrescos cold drinks

regalo gift; bargain

régimen diet

regulación control

remo oar

RENFE Spanish Railways (44)

reparaciones repairs

repostería cake and pastry shop; confectionery

repuestos spare parts

reserva booking

respete(n) observe! respect (i.e. don't damage)!

retirada removal

retirar remove

revisiones checks, overhauling

rey king

reyes king and queen, monarchs

rogamos we ask (i.e. please)

roja red

románico Romanesque

romano Roman

ropa laundry, clothes

ruedas wheels

ruta (tourist) route

S. = San; señoras; siglo; sur

S.A. = Sociedad Anónima Co. Ltd.

sábado Saturday(s)

sala hall, room; indoor

sala de fiestas dance hall

sala de juego amusement arcade

salida departure; way out, exit

salida de emergencia emergency exit

salón large room, hall

San (S.) Saint (male)

sanitario health . . . , medical

Santa (Sta.) Saint (female); holy

Santo (Sto.) Saint (male)

saquen buy! get!

sarcófago sarcophagus

se one (12)

se admiten we allow, are allowed

se alquila(n) 'to let'

se colocan we fit, are fitted

se hacen we cut, are cut; we make, are made

se permite(n) it is allowed

se prohibe it is forbidden

se revelan we develop, are developed

se ruega it is requested, you are requested, please (6, 11, 12)

sección department

seco dry

sector sanitario medical room

seguridad safety, security

Seguridad Social state health service

sellos stamps

semi-directo (sem.) type of train (44)

sentarse (to) sit down

sentido direction

señalización signposting

señora lady

señoras 'ladies'; (for) women; ladies

servicio service; duty; servicing

servicio de bomberos fire service; fire brigade

servicio farmacéutico dispensing service

servicios loos, toilets (86); services

servicios generales general servicing

siga drive on, continue

siglo (S.) century

sin without

sin salida dead end, cul-de-sac

sin servicio no service, closed

sírvase serve yourself

socios members

socorro emergency; help, aid

sol (in the) sun

solamente only

sólo only

sombra (in the) shade

sortida exit (Catalan)

sótano basement

Sra. = Señora

Sta. = Santa

Sto. = Santo

su(s) your

subida way up

subir to get on, board; to go up

suelo floor

super four-star petrol

sur (S) south

T = estanco; taxi

tabacos tobacco and cigarettes

taberna bar

tablao place where flamenco dancing is performed

Talgo (Pendular) type of train (44)

tallas sizes

taller(es) workshop(s); repair workshop(s)

tancat (tancada) closed (Catalan)

tapas bar snacks, snacks with drinks